The

TRAVELER'S GUIDE

to

CHINCOTEAGUE
& ASSATEAGUE

A SHORTCUT TO THE MAGIC

DAVID PARMELEE

SUNBURY
PRESS

Mechanicsburg, PA USA

Published by Sunbury Press, Inc.
Mechanicsburg, Pennsylvania

www.sunburypress.com

FIRST SUNBURY PRESS EDITION: February 2022

Set in Adobe Garamond Pro | Interior design by Crystal Devine | Cover by Lawrence Knorr | Photos by Darcy and Steve Cole, DSC Photography | Island Voices photos by Andrea Parmelee | Edited by Lawrence Knorr.

Publisher's Cataloging-in-Publication Data
Names: Parmelee, David, author.
Title: The traveler's guide to Chincoteague and Assateague : a shortcut to the magic / David Parmelee.
Description: First trade paperback edition. | Mechanicsburg, PA : Sunbury Press, 2022.
Summary: Author David Parmelee shares with you first-hand knowledge gained during many trips to Chincoteague and Assateague Islands with his family: what to do, where to stay, where to eat, and how to enjoy the local culture. An invaluable guide for planning your trip, and to uncover the magic of Chincoteague while you're there.
Identifiers: ISBN 978-1-62006-907-3 (softcover).
Subjects: TRAVEL / United States / South / South Atlantic (DC, DE, FL, GA, MD, NC, SC, VA, WV) | NATURE / Animals / Horses | NATURE / Ecosystems & Habitats / Coastal Regions & Shorelines.

Product of the United States of America
0 1 1 2 3 5 8 13 21 34 55

Continue the Enlightenment!

To my wife and family,

whose love is the magic of Chincoteague for me.

CONTENTS

INTRODUCTION: WHY I WROTE THIS GUIDE

Our Family's Experience   1

WHY GO TO CHINCOTEAGUE AND ASSATEAGUE?
THE APPEAL OF THE ISLANDS

The Delmarva Peninsula Region   5

The Island Feel   9

ISLAND VOICES: *Kirk Mariner—Local Historian*   11

Family-Friendliness   11

The Welcoming Southern Style   13

Locally Owned Business   14

THE FAMOUS CHINCOTEAGUE PONIES: STARS OF THE SHOW   15

Pony Origins   15

ISLAND VOICES: *John Amrhein, Treasure Hunter*   19

About Today's Chincoteague Pony Herd   20

ISLAND VOICES: Darcy Cole and DSC Photography   22

Pony Penning   24

Four Pony-Watching Strategies   27

ISLAND VOICES: *Denise Bowden, Chincoteague Volunteer Fire Company and
Chincoteague Town Council*   32

CHINCOTEAGUE CULTURE   35

Watermen, Seafood, and Oysters   35

ISLAND VOICES: *The Chincoteague Volunteer Fire Company*   36

Seafood Today   38

ISLAND VOICES: *Captain Chandler's Cemetery: (Lightning and Biscuits)*   38

ISLAND VOICES: *Tim Dring, USN (Retired) USCG Volunteer Historian*   39

WHAT TO DO   41

Sunsets over the Chincoteague Channel   41

Spots for Sunset-Watching   43

The Farmers and Artisans Market   43

The Assateague Lighthouse   44

The Museum of Chincoteague Island   44

ISLAND VOICES: *L. Bryce Van Stavern, Museum of Chincoteague Island* 46
ISLAND VOICES: *Russell Fish, Decoy Carver and Board Member of
  The Museum of Chincoteague Island* 48
Chincoteague Step through Time Tours 49
ISLAND VOICES: *Cindy Faith, Chincoteague Step through Time Tours* 50
Festivals 51
The Island Theatre and the Chincoteague Cultural Alliance 57
ISLAND VOICES: *Lexi Hubb, Chincoteague Cultural Alliance and
  Chincoteague Island Theatre Company* 57
The Wallops Flight Facility 59
ISLAND VOICES: *Keith Koehler, Wallops Flight Facility News Chief* 60
ISLAND VOICES: *Amy Barra, Wallops Flight Facility Visitor's Center* 62
The Captain Timothy Hill House 63
Shopping 64
ISLAND VOICES: *Jon and Jane Richstein, Sundial Books* 68
ISLAND VOICES: *Erick Sahler, Erick Sahler Serigraphs Co.* 69
Shells 71
Fishing: Channel and Offshore 72
Campfires and Stargazing on the Beach 73
Maui Jack's Water Park 74
Bicycle and Bike Rentals 74
Kayaking and Canoeing 76
Clamming 76
Birds 77

THE NATIONAL SEASHORE AND THE CHINCOTEAGUE NATIONAL WILDLIFE REFUGE ON ASSATEAGUE
The Natural Environment 87
The National Seashore: Non-Commercial ... with PARKING! 89
Dogs 94
Trash on the Beach 97

WHERE TO STAY
National Chains 98
Local Hotels, Inns, and Bed-and-Breakfasts 99
The Rental Picture 102
Locations and their Advantages 107
Camping 110
Staying Off the Island 112
ISLAND VOICES: *Ruthann Mason, The Waterside Inn* 113

WHERE TO EAT

Local Restaurants: Brick and Mortar   115

ISLAND VOICES: *Tom Clark, Don's Seafood Restaurant and Tom's Cove Aqua Farms*   119

Sea Star   120

Food Trucks: Many and Varied   121

ISLAND VOICES: *Larry Parsons, Woody's Serious Food*   122

Cook-it-Yourself and Takeout   129

Baked Goods and Ice Cream on Chincoteague   135

ISLAND VOICES: *Jerry and Paula Alms, Church Street Produce*   136

The Great Ice Cream Debate: Island Creamery vs. Mr. Whippy's   138

ISLAND VOICES: *Kelly Conklin, Island Creamery*   140

ISLAND VOICES: *Drew Conklin, Island Creamery Berlin and Salisbury*   142

Where's the Bread?   143

Black Narrows Brewing   144

Where to Wine?   145

The Caffeine Scene   145

*2021 Reviews   147

How to Shuck and Eat an Oyster   147

You Really Should Know About Country Ham   149

LOGISTICS

Routes to the Island: by Car   151

Routes to the Island: by Air   151

Health Care   152

Dentists   152

Closest Off-Island Resources: Pocomoke and Salisbury   152

Groceries: On-Island of Off?   153

What to Bring Hiking, Birding, and Pony Watching: Binoculars, Guides, and Bug Stuff   153

Equipment Rentals: Umbrellas, etc.   156

Car Trouble   156

RV Trouble   157

ISLAND VOICES: *Chief R. K. Fisher and Captain Tyler Greenley, Town of Chincoteague Police Department*   157

ISLAND VOICES: *Jack Tarr, former Mayor of Chincoteague*   158

ACKNOWLEDGMENTS   160

ABOUT THE AUTHOR   161

GOD ALSO SAID: Let the waters that are under the heavens be gathered together into one place: and let the dry land appear. And it was so done. And God called the dry land, Earth; and the gathering together of the waters, he called Seas. And God saw that it was good.

. . . and God created the great whales, and every living and moving creature, which the waters brought forth, according to their kinds, and every winged fowl according to its kind. And God saw that it was good. And he blessed them, saying: Increase and multiply, and fill the waters of the sea: and let the birds be multiplied upon the earth.

The opinions expressed in *The Traveler's Guide* are my own. I haven't been compensated for them. If you patronize a business because of what you read here and are happy with your choice, I'm happy, too. There are so many good things about Chincoteague. I may have left some out. I apologize for any errors and omissions and will strive to correct them whenever possible.

WHY I WROTE THIS GUIDE

W HAT WOULD AMAZE the Founding Fathers most if they could see 21st century America? Perhaps this: most of us carry a small device that gives us access to all the knowledge accumulated in the history of mankind—and we use that device to argue with strangers and share pictures of cats.

Our phones do everything now, including Facebook rants, cat photos, and much of what books used to do—especially guidebooks such as this. You don't need me to tell you where the nearest hospital to Chincoteague is located (I've included two, just in case). A search takes seconds. Online reviews of Island hotels and restaurants number in the hundreds, even thousands, on well-known sites like Yelp and TripAdvisor. So, why this guide?

First, to help you find direction. When we search, we often aren't sure of the destination. There's no substitute for knowledge gained by walking around a place for many years. Why re-invent the wheel, doing hundreds of searches on accommodations, things to do, food and drink, Island culture, and the national seashore? We've done the searching in person. We've stayed on the Island, enjoyed the food, shopped at the stores, and experienced the natural environment.

Second, I want to share my experience of Chincoteague in hopes it will help you find the magic you're seeking there. From the start, you'll have one person's opinion on everything I write about, so you can make better choices for yourself and your family.

· OUR FAMILY'S EXPERIENCE ·

I should warn you that I am NOT objective about Chincoteague. I love the place. I believe you will, too. I will always be honest—even about my biases.

Four generations of our family have visited Chincoteague and Assateague—three of them many times. My wife and I first came as birders. We lived in Philadelphia and had already spent time in Brigantine, Cape May, and Bombay Hook (The latter, in Leipsic, Delaware, is 115 miles from Chincoteague). We heard what a fine birding spot the Island was, especially during migration, and made the trip in 1983, before we had children, spending most of our time at the Refuge on Assateague. The ponies roamed freely then. We recall signs warning us not to pet them because they carried poison ivy residue on their coats. That seemed a bit far-fetched, but the advice was sound. They are wild animals. A bite or kick from a startled pony can do great damage. We will admit to giving a quick pat to a particularly docile and friendly mare who approached us.

We learned about Sika deer, small compared to our Pennsylvania whitetails, and the charming Delmarva Fox Squirrel. We watched skimmers, oystercatchers, ibis, egrets, herons, osprey, terns, and many, many shorebirds. We left happy, with a resolve to return.

And time passed. We welcomed three children into the world. We moved two hours farther north, to Northeast Pennsylvania, where we were born. We were both busy working and raising a growing family. Vacations were short and kid-focused. We didn't get back to Chincoteague.

One day in 1996, my wife resolved to go to pony-penning. Our son was eleven, our older daughter was six, and our younger daughter was just one year old. Well into her seventies, my wife's mother decided to come along with a close family friend who often cared for our kids. I had work commitments, but the large group led by my wife set out in a rented Ford minivan. The closest accommodations were in Crisfield, Maryland, "The Crab Capital of the World," an hour away. They made it to the Channel in time, survived the melee, and had fun; my wife hadn't realized how much close contact with marsh mud was involved. She recalls that her mother's hairdo, always perfect, didn't fare well in the warm, humid environment. It wasn't our one-year-old's favorite day. Grandma spent a lot of time holding her. They returned with good memories. The seed planted over a decade earlier had sprouted.

Fast forward to 2005. We'd been blessed with a second son, six years old then. With four active kids, we had acquired a GMC Suburban. We mounted a Yakima carrier and took off for our first vacation rental home. With us was the daughter of a close friend of my wife's. She and our older daughter became good friends and would prove great traveling companions. At that point, we had never stayed on Chincoteague. When I picked up our keys from Bill Cherrix at Island Getaways, I asked what we should plan to do. "Just go the beach," he advised breezily. We did, often, re-discovering the charms of the Island and learning new ones. As Humphrey Bogart said at the close of *Casablanca*, it was the beginning of a beautiful friendship.

Since then, we've returned a dozen times, staying in as many different homes and hotels. I've published a historical novel set on Chincoteague (*The Sea Is a Thief,* Sunbury Press, 2013), researched at the Island library. I've had the honor of speaking about the book at the Museum of Chincoteague Island. In 2020, Lexi Hubb and the Chincoteague Island Theatre were kind enough to stage a reading of my one-act play set on Chincoteague, *Home and Contents,* on the breezy veranda of the Chincoteague Cultural Alliance.

Our whole family's relationship with Chincoteague has deepened and expanded. The six-year-old whom Captain Daisey let steer his tour boat under the Assateague Bridge is now 22. He's brought the love of his life to the Island. Our older daughter and her husband have a child of their own, who played with the tendrils of a stuffed jellyfish, lying on her back on the sofa at three months. She's a Chincoteague veteran now, with three visits to her credit. She has no fear of the ocean and truly loves Toddler Beach in Tom's Cove and Veteran's Memorial Park. She polished off a chunk of crab cake at age two. She even has her own Soft Pony.

We've taken to renting the same home. Each year, on arrival, we hang our hats on the rack inside the door—beach hats, straw hats, and a Sundial Books or Museum of Chincoteague Island ball cap. We line up our shoes underneath: Birkenstocks, Chaco's, water shoes, Crocs. Some very little shoes have joined the bigger ones now.

Each year, for a brief, blessed time, Chincoteague is where we hang our hats. For the rest of the year, a piece of it remains in our hearts.

I want to share that with you. I want to help you prepare so your trip is easier, and assist with logistics, so your time there is unencumbered. I want to share the discoveries we've made in the last 25 years and let you in on some secrets. I want to provide direction so you can follow your bliss without obstacles. In short, I want to offer you some of the treasures we've discovered on the Island. If I can accomplish that, your happiness on Chincoteague will be all the greater—and so will mine.

Godspeed, friend! Let's go to Chincoteague and Assateague.

(Photo by Darcy and Steve Cole, DSC Photography DSCPhotography.net.)

WHY GO TO CHINCOTEAGUE AND ASSATEAGUE? THE APPEAL OF THE ISLANDS

· THE DELMARVA PENINSULA REGION ·

The attractions of Chincoteague and Assateague are easy to discover and understand. The wild ponies, of course, a unique Island treasure; the unspoiled and undeveloped beach; the unrivaled seafood—and, recently, an exploding food scene in general. Scenery. Birds. Sunsets. And a singular brand of relaxation.

There's way more to the region than that. The Islands are part of a marvelous section of the U.S., well worth exploring. Local historian Kirk Mariner (1943–2017), author of many books on the area, put it particularly well:

> The Eastern Shore of Virginia—detached and sometimes
> forgotten by the rest of the state, is a pleasant rural place where
> life is noticeably slower and more relaxed, though the distance
> to the great cities of the Northeast is not great . . .

The Eastern Shore, sometimes known as ESVA, is part of a larger landmass, the Delmarva Peninsula, made up of parts of the states of DELaware, MARyland, and ViginiA) extending southward from mid-Delaware to Cape Charles, Virginia, like a forefinger pointing to the floor from a clenched fist: 6000 square miles, 2600 miles of coastline on two bays and an ocean. No spot on it stands more than 400 feet above sea level.

In Philadelphia, you're definitely in the Northeast, only an hour and a half from Manhattan by train. Wilmington, Delaware, a smaller cousin of Philly located just south of it, is a Northeastern city. As you make your way south through the midsection of Delaware, the picture begins to change. Multi-lane highways, clusters of box stores, and industrial centers give way to a different landscape.

Travel just forty miles from Wilmington to Smyrna, Delaware, and a brief eastward detour will lead you to the Bombay Hook National Wildlife Refuge, a crucial stop on the Atlantic Flyway for migrating birds. Each spring and fall, you'll spot thousands of shorebirds on the expanse of tidal mud flats within the refuge (Bombay Hook is a fine day trip for birders, worth a stop). Soon, you'll begin to see road signs with the most welcome word we know: BEACHES. In just over an hour, you'll cross into Maryland and then Virginia before you know it.

That's Delmarva. Close to a million people live there, but they like to leave a little space in between them—for comfort, y'see. Wikipedia, master of plain speaking, puts it this way:

> The culture of Delmarva is starkly different from the rest of the Mid-Atlantic region and is much like that of the Southern United States. While the northern portion of Delmarva, such as the Wilmington, Delaware metro area, is similar to the urban regions of Philadelphia, the Maryland and Virginia Delmarva counties (as well as the southern two counties in Delaware) are more conservative than their "mainland" counties.
>
> Delmarva is driven by agriculture and commercial fishing. Most of the land is rural, with a few large population centers, though tourism has been an important part of the region . . .

The folks at Wikipedia don't use many adjectives, but their meaning is clear. Delmarva has a culture all its own, inspired by geography but maintained by people. From time to time, most recently in 1992, somebody has started a local movement encouraging the various counties in the region to secede from their home states and create the "State of Delmarva." When you're there, you can see why.

The Chesapeake Bay acts as a divide between the Peninsula and the rest of the country. No bridge spanned it until 1952. It's no wonder Delmarva residents feel a deeper connection to their neighbors on the Peninsula than to their respective states. During a recent visit to Chincoteague, one area resident referred to the "Western shore of Virginia"—that is, the part of the state facing the Chesapeake Bay rather than the Atlantic Ocean. It's a different perspective, to be sure.

As you pass sprawling corn and soybean fields off Route 13, watered by giant, centipede-like precision irrigation systems on stout tractor tires, you'll understand the agricultural way of life in the region. When you watch watermen head out each day for fish and prized blue crabs, you'll understand the economic importance of the Chesapeake Bay way of life. By the simple act of traveling there to enjoy what the Peninsula has to offer, you'll help sustain families who depend on tourism. They're happy to see you and glad to let you know.

Speech, accents, and colloquialisms change as you travel down the Peninsula, too. Again, our friends at Wikipedia: "It has been suggested that Delmarva residents have a variation of Southern American English which is particularly prevalent in rural areas . . ."

"Suggested?" If you've been there, you know that for a fact. If not, listen to Mayor James "Ooker" Eskridge of Tangier Island, Virginia (among the most isolated places in the United States), discussing the COVID pandemic on YouTube. He handled it well. But who do you know who sounds like him? (Hint: you don't know anyone unless you live on the Eastern shore). https://www.youtube.com/watch?v=6vaGOXebcZc

The Standard American speech of news anchors, sitcoms, and commercials, beamed into every household via television and the Internet, will no doubt bring this distinctive regional speech an end—someday. Not yet, though, and that's a good thing. Chincoteaguers have their own speech, unique in the American soundscape. A visitor may have difficulty keeping pace with a 'Teaguer's conversation. Conventional wisdom says Southerners talk slowly. They talk as fast as anyone. They just have a different sense of pace and rhythm.

The Eastern Shore of Virginia is a unique place in a unique region. Chincoteague is the pearl in the center of that oyster. It lies about two-thirds of the way down the Delmarva Peninsula, between the second and third knuckle of that downward-pointing finger. In the past, it's been spelled Gingoteague or Gingoteek, after an Algonquin tribe that lived on the Island. As late as 1872, the post office was listed as "Gingotig," according to area language expert Ryan Webb. Locals pronounce the name of their island "SHINK-o-tig," which makes perfect sense in light of that. I learned recently that the translation of "Chincoteague" from Native American languages is not "beautiful land across the water," as we're usually told, but the more prosaic "large inlet." The poetic translation originated in the 20th century. "Beautiful land across the water" describes the place so perfectly. It's the motto of the Town of Chincoteague, and a fine one, whatever its origin. I wish I'd thought of it.

"Across the water" is a given. Before constructing the four-mile Chincoteague Causeway, a series of six roads and low bridges built in 1922 to connect various creeks and inlets between the mainland and the Island, visitors could reach Chincoteague only by boat. The wooden billboards now spaced at perfect intervals along the causeway are many a family's landmarks (ours included): an unspoken signal to roll down the windows and take in the heaven-sent aroma of marsh mud. It means you've finally arrived in a beautiful place.

What makes it so beautiful? Why does the causeway inspire that treasured ritual for so many? Beauty is in the eye of the beholder; what do we behold as we roll across that causeway, built on tidal marshland and shifting sandy soil?

Some of the appeal of Chincoteague lies in the mental landscape. Because of the nature of the place, we see things differently there. The taste of a wine enjoyed with friends lingers on the memory as better, perhaps, than the wine actually was. So, with the beauty of the Island of Chincoteague and Assateague—some of it lies in associations.

Still, the Island is undeniably beautiful. It's surrounded by mudflats and marshes that host thick swaths of native grasses, pale green and yellow, yielding in unison to the bay breeze. Tall, graceful wading birds—herons, egrets, and ibis—stalk them with long, pointed bills. Dolphins cruise the channels, dorsal fins arcing into the air, then disappearing again, as brown pelicans crash-dive for fish nearby, black-hooded laughing gulls trailing in their wakes.

The famous ponies graze on the wild stretches of land in bands of two, three, or a dozen, their trademark patterns making them identifiable on sight. Tall loblolly pines share terrain with maples, oaks, persimmon, and sassafras, while crepe myrtle and wax myrtle lend a more delicate elegance to the undergrowth. Osprey and eagles soar silently on six-foot wingspans over creeks and pools in search of a meal. On a clear day, the blue dome of the sky, punctuated by the whitest of clouds, seems infinite. Even an approaching storm brings a darkly ominous grandeur. And, of course, there is the Atlantic Ocean itself, a friendly timpani thundering against the undeveloped shore of the barrier island of Assateague, offering up the gift of shells for those who know where to look.

The beach on Assateague is never this empty, but always this lovely. (Photo by Darcy and Steve Cole, DSC Photography DSCPhotography.net)

Against this natural canvas, 3,200 residents of Chincoteague Island have built their homes and businesses. Most sit lightly on the landscape, often following a traditional "waterman's cottage" design, a simple and quietly compatible wood-framed two-story home at peace with its surroundings. On busy Maddox Boulevard, the focus of the most activity now, clusters of businesses, signs, and parking lots combine for a feel of fun clutter; travel only a block either way, and that fades to the look and feel of a small Southern town going about its business. On some streets, bicycles are as common as cars.

You may know of a more welcoming and pleasant place to spend some idle time. I don't. Perhaps that's the greatest part of its beauty.

· THE ISLAND FEEL ·

People born and raised on Chincoteague often comment on how much it has changed over time. Before the construction of the causeway in 1922, the need to take a boat to the Island kept visitors to a minimum. It was a destination for waterfowl hunters and fishermen, but few others. Even into the 1960s and 1970s, visitors were comparatively few. The ratio of from-heres (native residents) to come-heres (more recent arrivals) was high. Photos of Main Street from that era reveal a typical small town: banks, barbershops, furniture and appliance stores, a Western Auto, and a car dealership (right where the old swing bridge stood). Fishing vessels large and small lined the waterfront on the channel side, a big part of the visual landscape of Chincoteague.

Pony Penning has attracted tourists for almost a century. Still, the number of seasonal visitors, and businesses that serve them, has grown rapidly in recent years. I bought a clam rake at Parks Hardware on Main Street in 2005. The store became a T-shirt shop the next year, as many local retail locations have. Chincoteague decoy carver Russell Fish said, "If you can't find a T-shirt on Chincoteague, something's very wrong." (There's still a locally owned Ace Home Center on Maddox Boulevard. They stock clam rakes.)

The economy of today's Chincoteague is overwhelmingly tourism-based. The days when it thrived on fishing and shellfish (the 19th and early 20th century) and chicken farming (the 1920s until the disastrous Ash Wednesday storm of 1962) are long gone. The standard article about the Island in national media no longer features the phrase "Best-Kept Secret." Thanks to enthusiastic word of mouth and the power of social media, Chincoteague is no secret. From Memorial Day to Labor Day (and even afterward, recently), the Island is busy. Still, Chincoteague has transitioned from a traditional Southern town to a "beach town" exceptionally well. It isn't like Martha's Vineyard or Cape Cod. It isn't like New Jersey beach towns "down the shore" or bustling weekend destinations on the Delaware coast. It isn't even like nearby Ocean City.

Are there lines at popular dining spots? Sure. They can be pretty impressive on occasion. Is there traffic on the causeway or the road to the beach? Naturally—at obvious times. Finding accommodations can be challenging or even impossible during peak season without planning. (Pony Penning week brings its own level of demand. It is not to be attempted on impulse). Still, Chincoteague is a place like no other. Though long-time residents find it very different from a few decades ago, it has maintained an elusive small-town feel and unique local culture and attitude that draws us back to the Island again and again. Yes, it is "Virginia's only resort Island." It is also the world's only Chincoteague. That's why legions of loyal fans declare it "my happy place." We live, and walk, and breathe, differently there. If you're planning your first trip, you haven't experienced that feeling yet. You will.

KIRK MARINER—LOCAL HISTORIAN

There's no better resource on the history and culture of Chincoteague and the Eastern Shore than Kirk Mariner (1943 to 2017). A Methodist minister who served six Virginia congregations, Mariner was a native of New Church, just off Chincoteague. His final resting place is in Greenbackville, the optimistically named town whose lights twinkle across the Chincoteague Channel when the sunset fades each evening. His books *Once upon an Island: The History of Chincoteague, True Tales of the Eastern Shore,* and *Off 13: The Eastern Shore Guidebook* offer a window into an area with few people but many traditions. They're very readable. Mariner's work begins in the heart. They may be a little tricky to find elsewhere, but they're on the shelves at Sundial Books (Jon and Jane Richstein will gladly ship) and the Museum of Chincoteague Island.

Kirk Mariner signs some of his many books about Eastern Shore history at Sundial Books, Chincoteague. (Photo couresy of Jonathan and Jane Richstein.)

▪ FAMILY-FRIENDLINESS ▪

Chincoteague is truly a family-friendly destination. That's not easy to define. Having spent many, many weeks on the Island with our large family, I contend it's as family-friendly as a destination could be if your vacation goals align with its attractions. Why so?

Chincoteague is a place to enjoy nature, wildlife, the beach, very good food, fun shopping, and unique local culture in excellent accommodations. It's relaxed and uncrowded, as a rule. It's quiet. Traffic is usually minimal. Parking is easy. The beach is as accessible as a beach could be, and less crowded than most. Because it's part of the Chincoteague National Wildlife Refuge, the attractions of the natural seaside environment play a central role: its beauty, its birdlife and marine life, its varied plants, flowers, and trees, and the rhythm of its landscape. The seashore, as God made it, isn't filtered out of Chincoteague and Assateague in favor of development and commerce. Rather, it's embraced. Slow-paced boat tours, and exploration tours with opportunities to get off the boat and discover what's going on in the marsh, are a big local industry. Kayaks are everywhere, as are bicycles.

The availability of rental homes that accommodate larger families at reasonable prices is a big plus. They allow busy parents needing a break to structure their time and activities around the needs of young children. The takeout option for food of every kind, and the ability to prepare meals in a full kitchen, make mealtimes less stressful and the pace of the day more flexible. They keep the cost of the trip down, too. Town parks and trails provide no-cost recreation for little ones (well-protected against mosquitoes, of course!). The town of Chincoteague offers plenty of places to buy beach gear and anything else you need at normal prices. True, it's a "beach town," but 3,200 people who shop there daily make it their year-round home. Their legacy is one of community, hard work, and thrift.

All that said, The Island may not offer the vacation your family is looking for. Jonathan Richstein of Sundial Books, a lovely independent bookstore in the heart of downtown, tells me visitors have been known to stop in to ask, "What is there to *do* here?" It's a valid question. The usual "beach town" attractions are conspicuously absent. There's no boardwalk. While there is a water park (Maui Jack's, opened in 2019 on a former campground), even that is smaller and more low-key than many. There are no big amusement-park style rides unless you arrive during the Fireman's Carnival at the pony penning grounds, the weeks just before and after the big annual event (the carnival was canceled during 2020 and 2021 because of the COVID-19 pandemic). Funland on Maddox Boulevard offers mini-golf (there's another across the street), bumper boats, an arcade, a bounce house, go-karts, a bungee "launchpad," and a kid's climbing wall. A ropes course went up in 2021. We've enjoyed most of them. Still, Chincoteague is not Six Flags or anything like it.

"Low-key" is a good watchword for Island attractions, as might be expected for a resort town whose claim to fame is a herd of 150 wild horses. Though she died in 1972, Misty, the pony heroine of Marguerite Henry's 1947 children's book *Misty of Chincoteague,* is probably the most effective member of the Chincoteague Chamber of Commerce. "Without those ponies," a friend told me, "Nobody would ever go there." I disagree. Only someone who hadn't experienced the manifold joys of the Island would hold that misperception. Certainly, though, far fewer people would go if the ponies weren't calling out to them. Most of us heard about the ponies first and everything else afterward.

Chincoteague is home to several good bars, some featuring live local music, but there's no "bar scene" to speak of. They're fun places to enjoy a drink near the water. You won't find nationally known acts that draw big crowds. That's not to say local musicians aren't talented—they sure are. The venues featuring music are different from larger ones in other beachside towns.

The Island isn't close to any large population center, but it's fairly close to many in the mid-Atlantic. For most people, it's a substantial trip. Our granddaughter, an April baby, visited the Island three times before she was three years old. Bless her patient parents! They called us this year as we both drew close to our destination. We could hear a small but insistent voice from the car seat in the second row: *"I want you to get me OUT!"* After a few hours, it's tough for one so young.

Yes, there is less to do on Chincoteague. Is that a bad thing? So many visitors have come to know it as "my happy place." Most of us take a vacation to unwind—then rewind by planning things to do on vacation. That may work for you. But will you head home "unwound?" From Chincoteague, you probably will.

· THE WELCOMING SOUTHERN STYLE ·

Our first trip to Virginia from Pennsylvania was to take our daughter to school. She needed furniture for her dorm room. We stopped at Pier One Imports. The woman at the counter quickly greeted us and offered to assist. We politely declined, intending to browse first. She just wasn't happy until we let her help.

Something similar happened on Chincoteague this year. I stopped at the Ace Home Center on the traffic circle. A bearded gentleman who seemed to be the owner dropped what he was doing to offer assistance. You don't find that often where we're from (You also don't find a rack of rifles and shotguns, carefully secured with a cable, in a hardware store). "It's a Southern thing," people often say, and I truly believe it is personal attention and a willingness to spend time in actual conversation. It feels good. Thank you for being kind and welcoming, Chincoteaguers. I, for one, enjoy it quite a lot.

• LOCALLY OWNED BUSINESSES •

Few chain stores, or national chains of any kind, operate on Chincote-ague. Local business predominates. Isn't that a welcome thing? You'll find a McDonalds, a Subway, and a Ledo Pizza, along with a Family Dollar and a Dollar General (no surprise). That's about it for "chain" retailers and restaurants. When you shop or dine on Chincoteague, you're sup-porting a family business—some larger, some smaller, but local. I, for one, am glad for the chance to do that.

THE FAMOUS CHINCOTEAGUE
PONIES: STARS OF THE SHOW

T HE BELOVED PONIES: without them, the Islands of Chincoteague and Assateague would be just as lovely in their unique way. The glory of the sunset would be undiminished. The dolphins would swim, the egrets would hunt, the pelicans dive, and the eagles soar. Nonetheless, Chincoteague would not be Chincoteague without the ponies. Perish the thought! The ponies put Chincoteague on the map, first locally, then worldwide. Though by law they belong to the Chincoteague Volunteer Fire Company, who leases grazing rights on Assateague Island from the Department of the Interior, they belong to us all, in a way—at least those of us who love the Island. The ponies *are* Chincoteague. Let's consider why.

· PONY ORIGINS ·

How did they get here? You'll hear different accounts. I like them all. Stories involving pirates, or Spanish galleons, are the best sort of stories, aren't they? On barrier islands, such stories abound. Chincoteague is no exception. The most popular version goes like this: Around 1750, a Spanish galleon foundered on the coast of Assateague. Its cargo of ponies swam ashore, where the herd prospered and propagated into the Chincoteague ponies we know today, the descendants of those brave survivors.

I like the story. It's full of adventure and intrigue. The chain of events is certainly conceivable. The "Saltwater Cowboys" of the Chincoteague Volunteer Fire Company stand behind it. I'm not going to argue with them, especially when on the Island. They make the case that more than one Spanish galleon is known to have been lost on the nearby coast. The *La Galga*, shipwrecked in 1750, is one. The National Chincoteague Pony Association sides with the fire company, too.

The Saltwater Cowboys of the Chincoteague Volunteer Fire Company at work with a pony band. (Photo by Darcy and Steve Cole, DSC Photography DSCPhotography.net.)

Based on insufficient evidence, the National Park Service, on whose land the still-wild ponies graze, isn't going for it. It maintains the ponies were brought to the Island in the 1700s or even before but discredits the Spanish galleon story (leave it to the bureaucracy to make life sensible but dull), offering instead the theory that the ponies are descended from local livestock that was grazed on Assateague, where people made their homes until the mid-20th century, then were lost and became feral.

Marguerite Henry (1902 to 1997), the author of *Misty of Chincoteague* and fifty-eight more children's books about horses and other animals, was intrigued enough by the tale of the shipwrecked horses to travel to Chincoteague in 1946, where she wrote *Misty,* forever altering the destiny of the Island. Many of the facts surrounding 18th-century shipwrecks weren't widely known even at that time. Henry heard the story from Clarence "Grandpa" Beebe, a lifelong Chincoteague resident who became a character in the book in the form of a local legend. "Legends," asserted Grandpa, "Be the only stories as is true!" The legend of that shipwreck is memorialized in *Misty of Chincoteague.*

In 1983, John Amrhein Jr., along with colleagues, began his search for the site where the *La Galga*, a Spanish galleon described in the legend, was shipwrecked off Assateague, yards from the Virginia/Maryland

Band on the run. (Photo by Darcy and Steve Cole, DSC Photography DSCPhotography.net.)

border. Surprisingly, documents on file with the state of Maryland since 1908 contained far more specific information than the residents of Chincoteague themselves could share with Marguerite Henry in 1946. The captain of the wrecked ship filed official papers the day it happened—September 5, 1750. The crew survived. Over the years, Amrhein worked his way closer to the ship's resting place. He's certain he's found it. You can read about Amrhein's work in his book *The Hidden Galleon* (New Maritime Press, 2007) and a forthcoming book. He offers strong evidence for the case made by the fire company (see the "Island Voices" on Amrhein). Spoiler alert: the ship now rests on land.

The old saying known as Occam's razor is "the simplest explanation is usually the best." College-professor friends tell me that's not necessarily so, but there's some value to the idea. The Chincoteague ponies may have arrived in a simpler, less glamorous way.

Long before it was made a National Seashore in 1965, administered by the US Department of the Interior, the Island of Assateague (a landmass separate from the Island of Chincoteague) was home to an entire community: Assateague Village, known as such from about 1850. Residents were forced to leave beginning in 1922, when Dr. Samuel Fields of Baltimore purchased a large and strategic parcel of land, fenced it

Two foals. (Photo by Darcy and Steve Cole, DSC Photography DSCPhotography.net.)

off, and posted armed guards. Villagers could no longer reach the waters and oyster beds where they made their living. Over time, they left, some floating their homes across the channel to Chincoteague, where at least they had electricity. Many a Chincoteague home standing today was relocated there via water.

Before that, sheep and horses were kept routinely on Assateague. Those who believe the ponies are of local origin, not escapees from a ship, speculate they were allowed to graze on Assateague to avoid prevailing laws and taxes. The Volunteer Fire Company argues such livestock were too valuable to be left roaming out of view of their owners. On the other hand, it's also true people will go to great lengths to avoid taxes.

In either case, the livestock owners needed to corral them from time to time to count them and mark new foals and lambs as their property. "Pony penning" and the presumably slower-paced "sheep penning" were recorded in the first half of the 19th century. Howard Pyle, a visiting reporter and artist, charmed (though a bit repulsed) by the rustic nature of life on Chincoteague, described and sketched it in 1877. It's thought the practice dates back much farther, perhaps as old as European settlement on the Island itself.

So—Spanish galleon, or tax evasion? At this point, no more hard evidence is likely to surface unless further investigation is permitted, and that seems unlikely (see the ISLAND VOICES on Amrhein). Use your judgment and pick one. You may want to ask your kids first (Care to guess?). Wherever their ancestors came from, the wild Chincoteague ponies you'll see when you visit are magnificent and handsome creatures. Few like them can be found anywhere in the world.

Ronnie Beebe, a descendant of Grandpa Beebe (quoted in *Misty of Chincoteague*), pointed out the same inlet to Amrhein in 1983. The progression of its closure from the sea is visible in aerial photos. Nat Steelman shared with Amrhein in 1982 his father's story of *La Galga*. The elder Steelman, who worked at the Pope Island Life Saving Station in the early 1900s, was told timbers sticking out of the marsh belonged to the Spanish ship that brought the ponies to Assateague. Amrhein has seen evidence using his magnetometer as recently as 2014. He's heard accounts of silver Spanish "pieces of eight" tonged up by oystermen and has seen hand-wrought iron spikes found in the vicinity of the magnetic anomalies he observed.

Though Amrhein has concluded *La Galga* is buried in the inlet, he hasn't laid hands on its timbers. That would require permission to excavate. Any such operation would be hampered by international entanglements between the U.S. and Spanish governments, based on treaties dating to 1763 and 1857. "The US Fish and Wildlife Service denied a permit to verify the location," he told me, "On instructions from the Spanish Embassy."

Amrhein isn't optimistic about a search for the hidden galleon by the National Park Service either, though the ship lies on federal land. "They must know where it is," he told me. "I've given them the information." He's certain of one thing, though: the ponies you see today are, in fact, descendants of the Spanish ponies from *La Galga*. He lays out the basis for his convictions and takes on some of the contrary arguments in this 2016 article from OceanCity.com:

https://www.oceancity.com/assateague-pony-origins-easily-traceable

The Hidden Galleon by John Amrhein: https://thehiddengalleon.com/

· ABOUT TODAY'S CHINCOTEAGUE · PONY HERD

In their feral state, horses can live about 25 years. They breed at a year old. However the original Chincoteague ponies found their way to the Island, the beautiful creatures we see today are many generations removed from their ancestors. Yet, they graze in conditions much the same as their famous forbears. The greatest difference in their lives is the watchful care of the CVFC.

The Chincoteague pony was first recognized as an official registered breed in 1994. They'd been around a long time before that. Much sought after by people who love horses, it's a very specific sort. About 150 live on the Virginia side, in the care of the Saltwater Cowboys. Around eighty more roam the Maryland side, which comprises two-thirds of the land-mass of Assateague Island. Technically, those are "Assateague ponies." A thousand or more are with private owners around the country.

(Photo by Darcy and Steve Cole, DSC Photography DSCPhotography.net.)

Typically, fifty to seventy foals (83 in 2021, a count maintained by Darcy Cole, who hikes Assateague daily and is the first to see fifty to seventy-five percent of the foals) are born to the Chincoteague herd each year. These are auctioned at the famous Fireman's Carnival in July. While many successful bidders take ponies home, others become "buybacks"—that is, the money is donated to the Fire Department, and the foal is returned to the herd.

Chincoteague Ponies would be called horses if not for their small stature. It's not their fault. All wild "horses" graze on whatever is available—grasses, leafy plants, and so on. Horses are herbivores, meaning they eat only plants. When you see a horse in the wild (there aren't many these days, especially on the East Coast of the US), it's probably eating. They eat 18 hours a day. The rest of the time, they sleep. It's all they can do to keep nourished. Chincoteague ponies do the same. Their diet of tough grasses and marsh plants is not as rich, so they don't grow as large. As you can imagine, the ponies are tough: heavy, sturdy, and strong, about 13 to 14 hands (54 to 58 inches) high, measured traditionally from the ground to the withers (the base of the neck at the shoulders). As bluegrass musician Doc Watson put it, them's good horses—just on the small side. By "small," I don't mean small compared to other animals. Big stallions weigh up to 850 pounds. By comparison, a thoroughbred horse, as you'd see racing the Kentucky Derby, stands 15 to 17 hands (60 to 68 inches) high, while jumbo-size workhorses like Clydesdales (Budweiser or otherwise) can reach 18 hands—six feet tall at the withers.

Whatever their size, a Chincoteague pony is a lovely creature. Pony-spotting alone makes a trip to the Island a joy. They can be almost any color: Brown, black, palomino, bay (brown or reddish-brown body with "black points" on the tail, lower legs, and edges of the ears), and chestnut (dark reddish-brown). Pinto horses are very common: a combination of white and a second color, often in a distinctive patchwork pattern that makes individual horses easily identifiable. Pony guides, available at Sundial Books and other local stores, allow you to learn the names and characteristics of specific horses in the herd. Yes, they all have names, many of them colorful, given them by their buyback sponsors. The right to name the pony is all you're actually paying for with a buyback bid. The Saltwater Cowboys of the CVFC have their own nicknames for some of the ponies—or so I hear.

+ The Chincoteague Pony breed: https://www.allhorsebreeds.info/
+ Chincoteague Volunteer Fire Company: https://cvfc3.com/pony-info
+ Sundial Books: 4065 Main St., Chincoteague, VA 23336 (757) 336-5825 https://www.sundialbooks.net/

ISLAND VOICES
DARCY COLE AND DSC PHOTOGRAPHY

"I actually had a pony named Misty when I was young, in upstate New York," said Darcy Cole, "But in 2013, when I met the Chincoteague ponies and discovered they all had names, I caught pony fever." Since then, she's hiked 11,000 miles on Assateague, over 2,000 in 2021 alone, following the herd and watching for new foals to be born. "I've been the first person to see at least half of them," she told me. "Maybe three-quarters." It keeps her on her toes. "A mare's labor takes only about twenty minutes. Within an hour, the foal tries to stand. It usually takes a couple of the tries, but within two hours, they're running in circles around their mothers." As everyone should, Darcy always keeps her distance, so the ponies aren't disturbed. They have become so accustomed to her they often show no concern even with a new foal sleeping at their feet. "I'll be watching a mare thinking she hasn't foaled yet, and the ears of a new foal will pop up out of the marsh grass," she recounts. "I watch for all the signs of good health. I wait to see if it starts nursing. If I have serious concerns, I call the Volunteer Fire Company. The volunteers drop everything and respond to an emergency with a pony just like it's a 911 call for a human being."

Darcy had nothing but praise for the Saltwater Cowboys and how they care for the herd. "All the ponies get three vet checks a year. If there are problems, they bring the pony in for treatment. Before a cold snap or during a difficult winter, they make hay drops in the marsh. The mares are healthier and have healthier foals. About six percent of foals born to domestic horses don't survive beyond their first month. Among Chincoteague ponies, it's closer to four percent."

Darcy Cole of DSC Photography, the first to see most of the foals born on Assateague each year. (Photo courtesy of Darcy Cole.)

Both the Maryland herd on the Maryland side of Assateague Island and the Chincoteague Pony herd in Virginia must be kept within set limits. In Maryland, birth control measures are used; in Virginia, mares foal naturally, and enough young ponies are sold at the auction during Pony Penning to keep the herd at its limit of around 150. About two-thirds of the mares foal each year. "It's like popcorn popping," said Darcy. "The first foal is born in February, March at the latest. April has the second-most births and May the most. The numbers fall throughout the summer, with a few in August and September. The last foal usually arrives in November." Darcy saw 2021's eightieth foal born on September 15th and the eighty-second on October 4th. Yearlings are kept at the Fire Company's carnival grounds all winter. They're released as a group and then join a stallion's "band" during the year.

Darcy's husband, Steve, has been a photographer for thirty years. She's an excellent photographer as well. Each January, they publish an updated guide to the ponies, photographed from both sides for easy identification, and a separate guide to the new arrivals, foals born that year. It's a best-seller for boat tours (Darcy highly recommended a tour for getting a good view) or pony-watching with binoculars from the roadside.

Darcy and Steve also create pony calendars and various pony-related items like hats, shirts, notebooks, and magnets made in the US on the Eastern Shore whenever possible. All their photographs can be found online at the DSC Photography website and in several shops on the Island. The catalog is extensive, including Island birds, landscapes, gorgeous sunrises and sunsets, the lighthouse, and rocket launches from Wallops Flight Facility. Still, the ponies are so popular that Steve Cole has jokingly dubbed all their other photographs "Not-a-Pony." You'll find several very good photographers working on Chincoteague, with prints available in many retail shops. We enjoy the work of DSC Photography and are glad to feature their photos in the *Traveler's Guide.*

As you might expect, Darcy has gained an unusual insight into the nature and personality of the Chincoteague pony. "They're incredibly smart," she said. "And each one is very different. It's not like watching a field of cows. I'm sure cows are different, too, but the ponies communicate so well, even when they're off by themselves. They often use their ears. They express themselves silently, through body language." Experts in human communication make the same observation: our primary means of communication is body language. The tone of voice is the second. Our choice of words is a distant third. In that respect, we may be more like ponies than we realize.

As you might expect, a woman who's out on the marsh every day also has advice about dealing with the Island's ever-present bugs. "If you want to use a repellent, go with the maximum one hundred percent DEET," she advised. "But really, your best bet is a cool, lightweight, long-sleeved shirt, long pants, and a big hat with mosquito netting. Just cover up."

~~~

Steve and Darcy Cole, DSC Photography: www.PoniesInTheMist.com (books, wearables, and souvenir items) and dscphotography.net (photos)

▪ PONY PENNING ▪

"Pony Penning," the annual event when the ponies swim from Assateague to Chincoteague, is the best—and also perhaps the worst—day to be on the Island of Chincoteague.

Once a year, the "Saltwater Cowboys" of the Chincoteague Volunteer Fire Company corral the Northern and Southern pony herds that live on the Virginia portion of Assateague Island into a fenced enclosure not far from shore. The herds live and roam not far apart. Very pregnant mares and very young foals get a free ride in a horse trailer or waterborne barge, along with any ponies whose health might be questionable. It's a careful process, to be sure.

The organization PETA (People for the Ethical Treatment of Animals) has objected to the Pony Swim because "penning up wild ponies and auctioning off foals to the highest bidder is reckless." Verifiable records of Pony Penning (and Sheep Penning, until about a century ago) date back to the 1830s. The Chincoteague ponies have done very well in the care of the CVFC. Their wild life is not easy; that can be said of any wild creature. Ponies die of age, "swamp cancer" (equine pythiosis, still stumping scientists), and accidents. Three became trapped in mud in April of 2017. One was dead when CVFC personnel arrived. Another died under veterinary care. The third survived. Pony watcher Darcy Cole knows as much about the herd as anyone and observes the ponies up close on most days. She gives the Volunteer Fire Company high marks for their stewardship of the herd (See "ISLAND VOICES: Darcy Cole"). "What would be a better alternative?" she asked.

Two foals. (Photo by Darcy and Steve Cole, DSC Photography DSCPhotography.net.)

When no bridge connected the two islands, the ponies had to be swum across to get them to Chincoteague. The permanent bridge on Beach Road, constructed in the late 1950s, made the swim unnecessary: it became an easy matter to herd the ponies across the bridge, then down Maddox Boulevard. Somehow, though, no one could picture Chincoteague without the pony swim. It continued. Though it lasts only about ten minutes, it's by far the biggest event in the region. Only COVID and World War II prevented it.

Even Groundhog Day doesn't compare. Punxsutawney, Pennsylvania, where Punxsutawney Phil keeps his burrow, is home to 6,000 people. Each February 2, 40,000 come to see the groundhog see his shadow (or not). Pony-penning draws an astonishing 50,000 to Chincoteague. In 1927, just five years after visitors could drive there, the Pony Swim attracted 25,000 spectators to a tiny island about which few people knew.

You might certainly want to be on the Island for Pony Penning. It can be a bit of a trial. Depending on when the slack tide falls, you may have to be up early to board a shuttle bus. You'll join a large crowd of people (not very Chincoteague). It will be warm, and the bugs will be biting (completely Chincoteague). Depending on where you find a spot, you may be up to your ankles in marsh mud (entirely Chincoteague). It's an event like no other anywhere else in the world.

(Photo by Darcy and Steve Cole, DSC Photography DSCPhotography.net.)

Still, it might be the right time of the year to skip. Everything else we love about the Island is there the whole season. Why share that with 50,000 people? The Fireman's Carnival is in full swing well before and after the date, with its crab cakes and oyster fritters.

> INSIDER TIP:
> The ponies swim BACK to Assateague the Friday following the Wednesday swim to Chincoteague. And you know who comes to watch them? Not nearly as many people. About half as many, actually. You heard it right here, folks!

✦ Pony Penning (Chamber of Commerce Site):
https://www.chincoteaguechamber.com/pony-penning/

▪ FOUR PONY-WATCHING STRATEGIES ▪

AT PONY PENNING

The annual Pony Penning falls on the last consecutive Wednesday and Thursday in July: The Pony Swim on Wednesday at slack tide (the period right between the falling and rising tide), and the Pony Auction on Thursday, when the new foals are auctioned off. If you can find a good spot during the fifteen-minute swim or along the road, the herd travels to the carnival grounds; you can see them all for a short time, like a spectator at the Tour de France watching the race as it passes. Ponies are kept in a holding corral at the carnival grounds, where you can linger as long as you like. If the big crowds (and premium prices) of Pony Penning week are not for you, there are still three ways to observe Chincoteague ponies on the Virginia side: good binoculars, a "cruise" or boat tour, and a kayak (or canoe).

Decades ago, ponies would stroll out onto Beach Road any time, unrestricted. They wandered the Island of Assateague. If you were on foot, they might walk alongside you. Their federal custodians didn't want unwary visitors touching them—first, for the safety of the people, who might get kicked, and second for the safety of the ponies. Who knows what people might feed wild horses? A Snickers bar? They'd go for that, but it certainly wasn't good for them.

Nowadays, the ponies are penned onto grazing lands some distance from public roads and trails. You can't blame their caretakers for keeping them at a distance. They're wild creatures. In their feral state, they don't always mix well with visitors.

(Photo by Darcy and Steve Cole, DSC Photography DSCPhotography.net.)

ROADSIDE PONY-WATCHING

Fortunately for us, the ponies don't mind being observed and can often be seen fairly close, grazing in the marshes on the south side of Beach Road as it approaches the beach. Since that area is part of the Chincoteague National Wildlife Refuge, you'll need the daily or weekly pass ($10 or $25) to get there in your vehicle. If you're a bicyclist, there's no charge. Approaching the area, you can easily tell how many ponies are out by the number of cars pulled over onto the shoulder.

You'll need binoculars. Because ponies are so large (compared to a bird) and stay fairly still, you won't need a large objective lens as you would for birding. Any decent pair will do. Once you've begun to watch ponies, though, you'll probably be curious about the wading birds and shorebirds usually found nearby. If you're investing in binoculars for the trip, your best bet is a good 8 x 42 (eight times magnification, with a 42mm objective lens) or 10 x 42 (ten times magnification) pair that doesn't stress the budget. They'll get you a close-up view of all kinds of wildlife on the refuge, at the beach, or a channelside or bayside rental. You never know who'll drop by. One year we spotted a Northern Loon, typically associated with Maine and Minnesota, floating lazily in a small pond near Wildcat Marsh.

Pony-Watching Cruises, or Boat Tours (and Other Kinds)

Sightseeing "cruises" by boat, known as boat tours, are a cottage industry on the Island and an excellent way to see and learn a lot in a very short time. Large, comfortable, and stable pontoon boats are the watercraft of choice, captained by experienced local guides who can show you what the Island has to offer. The watercraft are inspected and certified by the U.S. Coast Guard, who are very serious about their work. The captains must be licensed. They're glad to provide their credentials.

Boats can be on the smaller side, or quite large, up to forty feet long. Some cruises have a general focus: island geography, birds, marine life, and, of course, pony-spotting. Some schedule around the setting sun for a memorable "sunset cruise." Others provide a more in-depth look at the ecosystem of the area. Kayak tours of the Chincoteague-Assateague channel are also available, even for the inexperienced, led by guides who seek the best opportunities to get very close to ponies, birds, and wildlife. On Chincoteague.com, you'll find a dozen or so captains offering cruises. They'll have much in common, but their different approaches will be easy to spot. Most visitors are after an up-close look at the ponies. While that's never a guarantee (the ponies set their own schedule), cruise operators know better than anyone where they're likely to be found.

(Photo by Darcy and Steve Cole, DSC Photography DSCPhotography.net.)

A cruise is the only way to get close unless you bring or rent a boat, kayak, or canoe and are willing to make the trek by water. You'll still want to bring binoculars for the best view. The cruise operator may even provide them (ask when you reserve). Birds of prey such as eagles and osprey are often another highlight of such a cruise, as are dolphins. If you're an experienced birder, you'll be looking for a variety of waterfowl, shorebirds, wading birds, and other coastal species.

Of course, enjoying the sunset from a unique perspective on the water is a good enough reason for a cruise all by itself. The captains not only know the Island; they know their guests. They're careful and considerate and more than capable of caring for their passengers, both adults and children. You can cruise with confidence.

What must the ponies think when big pontoon boats pull up several times a day to watch them going about their business? Eating grass in the marsh mud, swishing their tails at flies—it's not a very exciting life. Yet, humans want to watch them live it. Go figure.

Reserve your cruise well in advance to avoid disappointment. They are popular.

- Assateague Explorer: Curtis Merritt Harbor, Chincoteague, VA, 23336 (757) 336-5956 https://www.assateagueexplorer.com/ Email: info@assateagueexplorer.com

- Assateague Tours: 7512 East Side Road, Chincoteague, VA, 23336 (757) 336-6176 https://assateaguetours.com/ Email: snugharbor@verizon.net

- Barnacle Bill's Boat Tours: Curtis Merritt Harbor, Chincoteague, VA, 23336 (757) 894-3745 https://www.barnaclebillswildponyboattours.com/

- Captain Barry's Back Bay Tours: 6262 Marlin Street, Chincoteague, VA, 23336 (757) 336-6508 https://captainbarry.net/ Email: captainchincoteague@gmail.com

- Captain Dan's Around the Island Cruises: 4161 Main Street, Chincoteague, VA, 23336 (757) 894-0103 http://captdantours.premiumsitehosting.com/ Email: CaptainDan@CaptainDansTours.com

- Chincoteague Island Adventures: 4436 Williams Lane, Chincoteague, VA, 23336 (757) 894-5964 http://www.chincoteagueislandadventures.com/ Email: Chincoteagueislandadventures@yahoo.com

- Cowboy Cruise Company: Curtis Merritt Harbor, Chincoteague, VA, 23336 (757) 990-1414 http://www.chincoteagueislandadventures.com/ Email: Chincoteagueislandadventures@yahoo.com
- Daisey's Island Cruises: Curtis Merritt Harbor, Chincoteague, VA, 23336 (757) 336-5556 https://www.daiseysislandcruises.com/ Email: fun@daiseyscruises.com
- Island Queen Inland Charters: Curtis Merritt Harbor, Chincoteague, VA, 23336 (757) 336-3528 https://www.islandqueeninlandcharters.com/ Email: bigcfishin1@gmail.com
- JS Expedition: Curtis Merritt Harbor, Chincoteague, VA, 23336 (757) 894-5279 https://www.chincoteague.com/jsexpedition/ Email: jsexpedition@gmail.com
- Marshland Charters: Curtis Merritt Harbor, Chincoteague, VA, 23336 (757) 894-1627 https://www.chincoteague.com/marshland-charters/ Email: marshlandcharters@verizon.net
- Proud Mary Charters: Curtis Merritt Harbor, Chincoteague, VA, 23336 (757) 894-0771 https://chincoteaguecharters.com/ Email: pmcharter@hotmail.com
- Spider's Explorer: 3801 Main Street, Chincoteague, VA, 23336 (757) 990-4242 http://www.chincoteaguespider.com/ Email: spider@chincoteaguespider.com

The greater and the lesser lights. (Photo by Darcy and Steve Cole, DSC Photography DSCPhotography.net.)

GUIDED KAYAK TOURS

An excellent way to blend the experience of kayaking on Chincoteague with the expertise of an experienced guide is to book a kayak tour. Kayak rental and launch permit are included. Your guide knows the best destinations, can assess your group's ability, and will probably get you "up close and personal" to the wild ponies seventy-five percent of the time. The quiet, unobtrusive little boats don't even get much attention from grazing animals just yards away if you're lucky. Be honest with your guide about your ability and stamina. They can advise how to plan for a pleasant excursion, not an endurance contest.

- ✦ Assateague Adventures (mobile unit): 4163 Main Street, Chincoteague, VA 23336 (865) 317-2507 https://assateagueadventures.com/ Email: assateagueadventuresinfo@gmail.com
- ✦ Snug Harbor Kayak Tours: Snug Harbor Marina, 8536 East Side Road, Chincoteague, VA 23336 (757) 336-6176 http://chincoteagueaccommodations.com/id8.html Email: snugharbor@verizon.net
- ✦ Assateague Boat and Kayak Tours: 7512 Eastside Road, Chincoteague, VA 23336 (865) 894-2431 https://assateaguetours.com/

ISLAND VOICES

DENISE BOWDEN, CHINCOTEAGUE VOLUNTEER FIRE COMPANY AND CHINCOTEAGUE TOWN COUNCIL

Denise Bowden can claim a lot of "firsts:" first woman in the Chincoteague Volunteer Fire Company and its first female president. First woman to be certified as a firefighter on Chincoteague Island. First female fire truck driver and ambulance driver. First female chair of the Fireman's Carnival.

She's not the first generation of her family on Chincoteague, though. She's the sixth. She's also a councilwoman for the Town of Chincoteague.

She does all that outside of her full-time job.

Denise is busy. Super-busy, in fact. Thirty minutes into our conversation, she told me she could only talk a few more minutes. She had already filled me in on a lot of things. "Many people have heard how the fire company started," she said. "In 1924, after two devastating fires, some of the upstanding men of the town—it was only men at the meeting—decided to take action. They could only raise $5 or so. But things got better when they made Pony Penning, which had always taken place, into a fundraiser for the Fire Company." Denise ticked off the current state of firefighting and EMS on the Island: "We have some of the best fire trucks and ambulances on the East Coast. While the firefighters are still volunteers, a full-time, 24/7 EMS crew shares the building. We deal with all sorts of incidents year-round, from fishhooks in thumbs, to bike accidents, to cardiac arrests. Some of everything." The crew are happy in their new headquarters on Deep Hole Road. "The old firehouse is beautiful," said Denise, "But it became tight. Technology advances every year. Fire-fighting equipment and ambulances get bigger and more complex."

Five women currently serve with the one-hundred-member CVFC. Once volunteers have fifteen years in, they merit "lifetime member" status, even when no longer active. Many "saltwater cowboys" enjoy that status. Denise is still active after thirty years of service. You won't see her in the water during Pony Penning though she rides. "I'm the one on shore, talking

Denise Bowden of the Chincoteague Volunteer fire Company. Denise reminds us: Only trained, fire company and pony committee members should approach the wild ponies and even then, with great caution. They will bite and kick and will cause harm to people and themselves, and you should NEVER attempt to feed or get within 20 feet of a wild pony. (Photo courtesy of Denise Bowden, CVFC.)

with TV camera crews and reporters," she explained. The tensest moment in recent history was a sudden thunderstorm of biblical proportions in 2014. "I was on a walkie-talkie with the cowboys out on the marsh," she related. "There was lightning all around. They had all the ponies gathered together and had no choice but to swim them. We were very fortunate. No one was hurt."

Like most firemen, Denise believes the ponies have their origins in a shipwrecked Spanish galleon but sees merit in the lost-livestock theory. "There may be some of both," she said. "You can see the foreign lineage in our ponies."

Denise has seen a great deal of Chincoteague history in her lifetime and that of her family. "I remember Mom and Dad sitting on the porch talking about taking a vacation, and Dad pointing out that we lived in the best vacation spot in the world. Before World War II, it was all seafood here. In the 40s and 50s, when that industry declined, people followed the example of their neighbors on the mainland and raised chickens. Millions. The Ash Wednesday Storm of 1962 wiped that out. When God closed that door, he opened a window: The *Misty* movie hit, and people began coming here as tourists. That's where we find ourselves now."

As a member of the Town Council, Denise is grateful for the cooperative spirit in the Chincoteague government. "We work well together. We listen to one another and make every attempt to understand, even when we don't agree. The biggest issue is a septic system. We've been talking it about since I was a kid." The pace of development is another conversation. "We love our hotels. They're excellent and great stewards of the community. They're full all the time. But I wouldn't be unhappy if no more were built. There's only so much property on the water." Denise is very happy with the island's building height limit: "Thirty-six feet. That's it."

"I think a lot about what I'd like to say to visitors," Denise told me. "First, if you've never ridden a scooter before, practice at home before you get on one here." Good advice from someone who drives an ambulance. "Prepare to relax," she added. "It's a laid-back atmosphere for a reason. People don't come here for nightlife. They come here because they don't have to deal with things they normally do. I can walk my dog at 2 P.M. or 2 A.M. Doesn't matter. I love to travel, but I always love to come home. You can have a bad time anywhere, but if you relax and enjoy what's offered, you can even enjoy the wind in the trees here, like I'm doing on my porch right now. If you want some quality downtime, this is the place to get it."

Denise agreed Pony Penning is a wonderful but hectic time to visit. "Plan very well for a Pony Penning trip," she advised. Fall is just great," she offered. "The birds migrate through. The water is warm in September, even October, when it's a little more chilly. You can still swim, and it's so quiet."

"When I wake up on this date ten years from now," said Denise, "I'd like to see Chincoteague just like it is today."

CHINCOTEAGUE CULTURE

▪ WATERMEN, SEAFOOD, AND OYSTERS ▪

Chincoteaguers, or "Teaguers," are known as a tough lot, most making their living by hard work and tenacity. The economy of the Delmarva Peninsula, and certainly Virginia's Eastern Shore, is driven by farming and fishing even today. Farming and livestock were more important than fishing to Islanders' livelihoods for over a century, in the early days after the Island was settled. After 1800, there wasn't enough land to support a growing population by farming alone. The Island turned to the sea for income. There, the oyster was king. Fish can be found everywhere, but oysters are more selective. They're right at home on Chincoteague.

Since the first brave soul tried one, oysters have been crucial to human survival for many centuries. Huge mounds of discarded shells called "middens," dating to prehistoric times, have been discovered up and down North American coasts. One in Maine was measured at over two million square feet.

Oysters are good for you and can sustain you as well. They're high in protein, low in fat and carbs, and a really good source of essential minerals such as zinc, iron, and copper. Before artificial ice and refrigeration, oysters could travel with an army (like Napoleon's) in a barrel of seawater. They weren't just survival rations, though. People loved them—especially Americans. In the 1800s, all sets of fine china included an oyster plate. Every good restaurant served oysters, some a dozen ways. Chincoteague oysters gained an excellent reputation, especially in the wealthy cities of the north (Listen to Lexi Hubb's podcast *The Bivalve Trail*, and you'll come to understand the role one resourceful and courageous man, Thomas Downing, played in that). By the 1860s, oysters were being harvested in their wild state and farmed or cultivated in managed beds.

THE CHINCOTEAGUE VOLUNTEER FIRE COMPANY

All fire departments are to be honored and acknowledged for their lifesaving work. Bless them. Few have achieved the notoriety of the Chincoteague Volunteer Fire Company.

The Island of Chincoteague first purchased firefighting equipment in 1905 for the princely sum of $25—a used pumper; 25 years old. You can see it, lovingly restored, in the Museum of Chincoteague Island. It prevented serious fires until 1920 when a large blaze destroyed twelve homes and businesses. In 1924, residents gathered to organize the first Chincoteague Volunteer Fire Company. It began with less than five bucks, collected by "passing the hat." That's not surprising; Chincoteaguers put in long days on the water just to make ends meet a century ago.

To operate a fire company, they needed a fire truck. That carried a five-figure price tag. Someone had a brilliant idea: turn the traditional pony-penning event into a fund-raising enterprise. The first "modern" Pony Penning, with some of the carnival atmosphere of the current event, took place in 1924. It worked. The fledgling company could put some cash down and take delivery of the fire truck it needed.

It only got better from there. Within six years, the handsome brick fire station that still stands at the corner of Main Street downtown had been built, and more equipment was on the way. Everything was paid for by 1935. Pony Penning was a stroke of genius. The Fire Company bought 150 ponies, stallions and mares, planning to auction off foals annually. At first, they brought modest prices; their value rose dramatically with time. Today, Chincoteague ponies are among the most sought-after in the world. Twenty years ago, the average bid for a foal was a bit shy of $2,000. By 2015 it had climbed to $2800. The online auction in 2021 raised the bar to over $5600. "Buyback" ponies, purchased by an individual, then returned to roam with the herd, sold as high as $25,500. The entire auction, including donated items like quilts, took in $420,000, even without the week-long carnival with its Ferris wheel, oyster fritters (don't even get me started), and crab cake sandwiches.

The CVFC today occupies a spacious new six-bay building on Deep Hole Road. It made the big move from its long-time headquarters in 2019. Since then, the town has purchased the landmark property to preserve it while putting it to another good use.

Membership in the Fire Company and its "Saltwater Cowboys" is among the highest honors a Chincoteaguer can earn. Most serve for a lifetime.

~ひ~

Chincoteague Volunteer Fire Company: 5052 Deep Hole Road, Chincoteague, VA 23336 (757) 336-3138 https://cvfc3.com/

The oyster trade was lucrative and important. During the War Between the States, Chincoteague, like nearby Tangier Island, voted overwhelmingly to remain loyal to the Union, though Virginia had seceded. Whatever the politics of Chincoteaguers, secession would have meant economic ruin. The local economy depended on shipping oysters north.

The Island's prosperity increased after the war. New residents arrived, including African Americans seeking work and opportunity. A few affluent families built large homes, some of which stand today. More churches were built, and a larger school. The taller lighthouse, now a symbol of the Island, first shone its beacon in 1867. By 1875 Chincoteague had its first grand hotel, the Atlantic, three stories with a full-length porch, built on the spot where the Island Theatre now stands. During the 1906 season, its register showed guests from eight states.

By that time, the oyster trade was booming. Their impact on the Island's economy was many hundreds of thousands of dollars. Shucked oysters were shipped in the iconic cans so collectible today. "Fish factories" that produced fish oil and fertilizer from the menhaden plentiful in local waters prospered as well, but oysters were the cash crop that fed most Island families.

The waterman's life was anything but easy, as those who live it now can attest: their harvest, at the mercy of the seasons and the weather, was unpredictable. Even in good times, their income was modest. As the 20th century progressed, fishing and fish products overtook the oyster trade in economic value to Chincoteague, but the sea was still the Island's sustenance. When even that proved insufficient, Islanders took to raising millions of chickens, as was done on the nearby Eastern Shore. In a sudden weather-borne tragedy, the Ash Wednesday Storm of 1962 flooded the low-lying Island and its sprawling chicken coops. They would never return.

Duck hunters and sport fishermen had always come to Chincoteague and Assateague for guided outings. The addition of the causeway in 1922 attracted more. The 1947 publication of Marguerite Henry's *Misty of Chincoteague*, along with the new prosperity of the 1950s and 1960s and the establishment of the National Seashore on Assateague in 1965, were milestones in the gradual progression of Chincoteague to "Virginia's Only Resort Island," as it's known today. The film version of *Misty* drew public attention on a Hollywood scale to an island entirely unaccustomed to the spotlight. Visitors began to arrive in numbers previously unknown.

Many local hotels still operating today were built on Maddox Boulevard in the 1960s. By 1985, tourism brought in nearly $25 million a year, surpassing seafood as the Island's biggest industry. Ten years later, the figure was $100 million. Chincoteague had found a new destiny for the 21st century, but it was carried there on the strong backs of watermen.

· SEAFOOD TODAY ·

Many resort areas are renowned for seafood. Even in the modern age of refrigeration and incredibly fast transportation (ninety percent of all roses sold in the U.S. are grown in South America), the very best seafood is served close to where it swam. That applies to shellfish as well as fish. Go to the Gulf for shrimp, Maine for lobster, and Chincoteague and environs for oysters and crabs. Truth be told, a huge variety of fish and shellfish is harvested in Eastern Shore waters: oysters, blue crabs, clams, scallops, flounder, tuna, drum, striped bass, and sea bass. Most are available on the Island from fish markets, restaurants, and takeout. Crisfield, Maryland, on the Tangier Sound of the Delmarva Peninsula, claims the title of "Blue Crab Capital of the World." It's only an hour away. So many kinds of seafood are "local" when you're on Chincoteague. Oysters are far from the only player on Island tables—but they are surely the stars.

ISLAND VOICES

CAPTAIN CHANDLER'S CEMETERY: (LIGHTNING AND BISCUITS)

Twenty-one small cemeteries are maintained on the one-mile by seven-mile island of Chincoteague. At the northern end of Main Street, in a generous cul-de-sac, is a cemetery with a single grave: Captain Joshua Chandler (1829 to 1877). A large concrete slab with a small headstone marks the actual grave. A wooden sign marks the spot. Chandler served in the Union army during the War Between the States. He captained a schooner and an oyster dredger after moving with his wife and daughter to Chincoteague in 1872. His crew included his son. As the story is told on the Island, the boat was hit by lightning near Wallops Island. The captain was holding onto the ship's brass rail while offering his crew a plate of biscuits. He was killed. Each of the crew took a biscuit in his memory. One survives in a glass jar in the Museum of the Island of Chincoteague. Chandler's family returned to Delaware. He rests, we hope in peace, on Main Street. Leave a coin, or a shell, as a testimony to the persistence of memory. Tough people like him made the Island what it was. They still do.

TIM DRING, USN (RETIRED) USCG VOLUNTEER HISTORIAN

For years we've passed the white-shingled U.S. Coast Guard Station on Main Street, a little south of the historic downtown, with no idea what went on there. To the visitor strolling by, there's little sign of activity.

Tim Dring will correct that impression right away. Tim, a New Jersey resident and retired US Navy commander with 27 years of service and a background in port security and harbor defense, has served as a volunteer historian for the Coast Guard since 2008. "The USCG often gets shortchanged," he pointed out. "You don't find large bases with facilities like other branches have. We have few historians, too. We're working on that."

Tim Dring, US Coast Guard historian, enjoying some advanced waterborne technology in New York harbor. (Photo courtesy of Tim Dring.)

It turns out USCG Station Chincoteague is a very busy place. About forty full-time personnel are headquartered there. Morning and evening, every day, they suit up for the weather and go on patrol in forty-seven-foot boats. "I've lost count of my visits. I've gone out with the crews many times, in all conditions," said Tim. "Local fishermen and guides call routinely to get the word on conditions. Chincoteague is also a major node in the Rescue 21 system launched in the 1990s. A network of towers enables rescuers to locate emergency signaling devices used by boaters to find them quickly when they're in trouble."

The Coast Guard as we know it began in 1915, but its roots run deep in American history. Tim told the story: "Life-saving services on the coasts, the Gulf of Mexico, and the Great Lakes grew quickly in the early 1800s when thousands of immigrants with little money booked passage here on old, ramshackle packet ships. The captains were a mixed lot. Navigation was still inaccurate most of the time, and maps were crude. Lighthouses and buoys were few and far between. They didn't yet have Fresnel lenses like the one on display in the Museum of Chincoteague. Not many people, even seafarers, knew how to swim. If a ship hit a sandbar a few hundred yards from shore in storm conditions, the surf could cause it to break up, and lives would be lost. That happened hundreds of times in the 19th century." A few committed individuals spurred Congress to appropriate just enough money to equip unmanned boathouses in seaside communities with lifesaving equipment. "The key was given to a responsible citizen, the 'keeper,' who recruited the strongest volunteer crew he could. The best-known success was the *Ayrshire* wreck in 1850. Two hundred and one lives were saved," noted Tim. "But there were failures, too, because of distance or inexperience."

"After the Civil War, Congress went farther, allocating enough money to staff the lifesaving stations with crews. In 1878, the US Lifesaving Service was established, with nearly 300 stations on the coast and the Great Lakes. The 'keeper' was there 24/7. A crew of six to eight, enough to row a large boat through heavy surf, was on duty during the storm season, September through April. They were chosen by merit only, not the patronage system, and followed military discipline."

The wages of the surfmen were minimal, and their barracks, not even that: heat, plumbing, and electricity weren't the norm until FDR's Treasury Secretary, Henry Morgenthau, was forced to seek shelter at the lifesaving station after a storm brought his sailboat aground. He was appalled by the living conditions of the men who saved his life, and made speedy changes. "The crews were there out of a sense of duty," said Tim. "It was a calling. Each told himself, 'I need to do this!' We have records of families of surfmen going back generations. Their job required them to patrol the beach on foot in all weather, wearing oilskins and carrying a kerosene lantern. A network of stations could call on one another for help. New Jersey had 42. Delmarva came close to that. The old abandoned lifesaving station you can see on Assateague dates to the 1920s. It replaced one built in the 1870s."

The surfmen, said Tim, were certainly heroes. "They were guardian angels. They got no support when injured. They were not provided with health care, pensions, or death benefits, though they saved so many lives."

The Coast Guard Station on Chincoteague began as a building serving light-houses and storing buoys. In 1964 it took on its current role. "The mission changed from protection of commercial shipping to protection of the fishing fleet to the modern focus on recreational boaters. In every era, many lives were saved."

The greatest challenge to the Coast Guard in the 20th century was prohibition. "The USCG was ordered to interdict smugglers of now-illegal alcohol and to use lethal force," explained Tim. "What the higher-ups didn't understand was that the smugglers, in many cases, were blood relatives." The solution was to transfer the crews to distant areas, where they would presumably be shooting at strangers. "It was a very difficult time for the Coast Guard," Tim told me.

Tim is an oyster fan. He likes the Nova Scotia oysters he can get in New Jersey. "They have a perfect blend of sweetness and saltiness," he told me. He also appreciates the famous Chincoteague Salts and the watermen who bring seafood to the market every day. "Fishermen can tell stories that would amaze you," said Tim. "They don't make a lot of money. They do what they do because they love to fish."

We love them for that. The sea is unforgiving in many ways. Thank you for your service, United States Coast Guard, on Chincoteague and throughout our nation.

WHAT TO DO

· SUNSETS OVER THE CHINCOTEAGUE ·
CHANNEL

Californians know the sublime beauty of a sunset over the water. On the East Coast, such sunsets are harder to come by. The Island of Chincoteague is blessed with sunset views for all of its seven miles, thanks to the channel that runs between it and the mainland. On its north end ("up island"), homes have been built in most practical spots, windows facing the setting sun. On Main Street south of downtown, where waterside development is less feasible, homes on the east side of the street often have a clear view of the channel. If your vacation rental has a good view to the west, you're in luck. Few things can match a Chincoteague sunset

(Photo by Darcy and Steve Cole, DSC Photography DSCPhotography.net.)

for beauty and a calming end to the day. Plan to be doing nothing around that time. When conditions are right, the setting sun will turn to flame and meet the nearby horizon, painting the sky with reds, oranges, and purples before the colors dim and yield to the indigo of twilight, then night. The twinkling of lights in Greenbackville, just across the channel, serves as a magical coda to another Chincoteague sunset.

Don't time the event. We never have. It's brief enough, to be sure, but time extends itself while it happens, and the glow in the hearts of those fortunate enough to see it lasts a lifetime.

A Chincoteague sunset is a blessing to be shared, as routine as the earth's turning, yet as sacred as the lighting of a candle on an altar. Treasure those sunsets given to you and the people about whom you care. You'll take many pictures of them. They'll be lovely. Still, something will be missing from the most artful photo. It lives only in memory.

An important note for morning people: if conditions are right, a Chincoteague sunrise can easily match the glory of a Chincoteague sunset. Steve Cole, whose gorgeous sunrise photos featuring the lighthouse grace The Traveler's Guide, points out that many people can't tell which he photographed. You'll want to face east if you're pursuing a sunrise, of course. It does feel good to get up so early and witness an everyday miracle such as that.

(Photo by Darcy and Steve Cole, DSC Photography DSCPhotography.net.)

▪ SPOTS FOR SUNSET-WATCHING ▪

If your vacation rental offers a sunset view, especially from the upper floor, you're in luck. If not, you can choose from several spots along Main Street to set up a camp chair and watch the daily miracle. Robert Reed Waterfront Park in the heart of downtown (easily located by the Misty statue and the oversized LOVE chairs) is among the most popular. Picnic tables are provided. Chincoteague.com maintains three live webcams, one from the park.

▪ THE FARMERS AND ARTISANS MARKET ▪

On the grounds of the Chincoteague Cultural Alliance on Church Street, you'll find, on Wednesdays and Saturdays, what our two-year-old granddaughter calls the "Farmer Market," officially, the Farmers and Artisans Market. It's a good one. You'll find a wide variety of non-farmed items for sale, all local and regional: vintage, wooden, woven, carved, printed, painted, and thrown. How is that anything but good? Chincoteague is an hour from any place of any size. Anyone taking the trouble to rent a booth at the market and schlep their stuff there is committed.

The produce is exceptional. Among the outstanding farmers is Bratten Farms of Willards, Maryland, 90 minutes from the Island, a fourth-generation farm that grows in the ground under greenhouse-style shelters for an early yield. Their tomatoes, cantaloupes, and tropical melons were a rare treat in mid-July.

At the 2021 Farmers Market, I first discovered Tom's Cove Aqua Farms. Tom's Cove has been farming oysters and clams in the Assateague Channel since 1999. The man-made "beds" in which the oysters grow make no difference to the oysters. What they care about is the water. One oyster we served at dinner this summer showed in its shell the distinct grid of the steel framework in which they're raised.

We've visited many open-air markets in Pennsylvania and Virginia. This is a nice one, worth a stroll. It's very manageable. Even if it's warm, you'll do fine. Take your small children. There's always music. They're local and play for free. (Did you tip the band? You didn't?? Surely this was an oversight. Go tip them. Give your smallest child the currency. The smile on the guitarist's face will be worth it, all by itself.)

- Chincoteague Farmers and Artisans Market: Saturdays: May 29 through
October 30, 9:00 A.M. to 1:00 P.M.; Wednesdays: June 9 through
September 29, 9:00 A.M. to 1:00 P.M.; 6309 Church Street, Chincoteague,
VA 23336 https://www.chincoteagueca.org/
https://www.facebook.com/cifarmersmarket

▪ THE ASSATEAGUE LIGHTHOUSE ▪

Lighthouses are wonderful, old-fashioned things and serve as the setting
for many stories. Assateague's signature lighthouse is a fading red-and-
white-striped historical gem, completed just after the War Between the
States. It ran first on a whale-oil lamp and wasn't converted to electricity
until the 1930s. Climbing all 154 feet to the top is a favorite thing to do
on the Island (be sure you want to. That's a lot of stairs). The views are
incomparable. You're not that high up, but both islands are so flat you can
see an amazing distance. At the top of your climb, you're standing next to
the two high-powered rotating lights that still serve as a navigational aid for
ship traffic. Imagine how welcome those lights look to the ship captains.

The trail to the lighthouse, though short, has a reputation for very
high mosquito density. Be ready.

Official lighthouse hours are 9 A.M. to 3 P.M. on weekends, spring
through fall. There's no charge. The lighthouse was closed during the
COVID pandemic; call the Chincoteague National Wildlife Refuge for
updated hours.

- Chincoteague National Wildlife Refuge: 8231 Beach Road, Chincoteague,
VA 23336 (757) 336-6122 https://www.fws.gov/refuge/Chincoteague/

▪ THE MUSEUM OF CHINCOTEAGUE ISLAND ▪

One of the great things about the Museum of Chincoteague Island is
that there's nothing of monetary value in it. You won't find paintings or
sculptures by old masters, collections of medieval armor, or Egyptian
hieroglyphics. Instead, everything in its collections is a memory of day-
to-day Island life over the last two centuries. It's a museum of the real.

Not long ago, it was called the Oyster Museum. The legacy of oystering is well-represented, as you'd expect. The Museum's logo features
a sail-powered oyster boat; among the most charming souvenirs on
the Island are the coffee mugs for sale imprinted with replica antique

(Photo by Darcy and Steve Cole, DSC Photography DSCPhotography.net.)

oyster-can labels (The cans themselves are highly collectible and costly. You'll see many on display). There's far more to the Island than oysters, though, and all aspects of Island life are preserved in simple but eloquent displays.

The tiny old post-office sorting desk is there, as is a homemade "sneak skiff" used by outlaw gunners to hunt ducks for the market under the noses of game wardens. (An artist painted that boat for the cover of my novel set on the Island, *The Sea Is a Thief*). Like other decoys and waterfowl-related exhibits, the skiff was once housed in the now-defunct Island Waterfowl Museum, whose contents were sold at auction in 2013. Delbert "Cigar" Daisey, among the best-known Island decoy carvers, was in residence there for three decades. He passed away in 2017. He and other renowned carvers, including Ira Hudson and Miles Hancock, are well-represented in today's Museum of Chincoteague Island.

The Ward Museum of Wildfowl Art, part of Salisbury University in Salisbury, Maryland (about an hour from the Island), also displays a large collection of decoys, along with a great deal of other material related to waterfowl.

Among the most thoughtful and valuable efforts undertaken recently to preserve Island history and culture (along with the 2011 restoration of the Captain Timothy Hill House) was the 2018 relocation of the Miles

Hancock workshop to the grounds of the Museum. Hancock lived and worked only about a mile away. He was among the most prolific carvers, producing as many as 20,000 decoys in a "primitive" style. His workshop was moved to the museum's grounds and set on a new foundation close to the main entrance. It stands exactly as he used it until he passed away at 87 in 1974, complete with tools and an old-fashioned pot-bellied stove. In season, contemporary carvers often stop by to create decoys in that venerable space. You can watch.

The two most popular exhibits in the museum, which charges visitors just $5, are the original Fresnel lens from the Assateague Lighthouse and the remains of Misty (yes, THE Misty) and her foal, Stormy, preserved by a taxidermist. Personally, I can live without the taxidermy, but no doubt many enjoy it. The lens is fascinating. It's huge, stretching from floor to ceiling, and contains literally tons of beautifully crafted shaped glass. It was taken from the lighthouse when the original lamp was replaced with the current electric beam and found a home, thankfully, in the museum.

Stop by the museum, especially if you're new to the Island. After even a short visit, you'll look at the place in a whole different way.

♦ Museum of Chincoteague Island: 7125 Maddox Boulevard, Chincoteague Island, VA 23336 (757) 336-6117 https://chincoteaguemuseum.com/ Email: museumofci@gmail.com

ISLAND VOICES

L. BRYCE VAN STAVERN, MUSEUM OF CHINCOTEAGUE ISLAND

"We like to ask people how they found out about the Museum of Chincoteague Island," said Bryce Van Stavern, its director. "Ninety percent say they were just driving by. That tells us we've got a great location (just before the bridge to Assateague on Beach Road), but we'd really like it if they knew about us before they came to the Island so they could plan a visit."

The Richmond native is relatively new as the director but not new to the museum world or Chincoteague. "Like so many people, we've been visiting the Island for many years," he told me. He's built a career in museums, working with visitors, managing, and training. Bryce served as Visitor Services Supervisor at the Museum of the Confederacy, now part of the American Civil War Museum, and was an interpreter at Colonial Williamsburg. He understands the role museums play in telling the story of a place and its people: "This little island that has survived over the years, moving from farming, to seafood, to poultry, and now to tourism." The Museum itself has a long history, still developing. "It began in 1972 as the Oyster Museum," Bryce noted. "There's only one other museum in the world dedicated to oysters. It's in France. The history preserved here was that of watermen, the oystering industry, and the Island's reputation. In the 1990s, its mission expanded, and it became the Oyster and Maritime Museum. We took on our new name, The Museum of Chincoteague Island, in 2010."

Bryce VanStavern, Executive Director, Museum of Chincotague Island, with the Fresnel lens from the old lighthouse.

Misty and Stormy, and the Beebe ranch, are well-represented in the Museum. Both Misty and her foal are present in person, thanks to the efforts of a taxidermist. "It's both our coolest and strangest exhibit," Bryce told me. "People show a wide range of reactions. Some are close to tears; others won't go inside. It's most exciting for kids. Every year, new young people discover reading, and with it that classic story, just like they discover baseball or anything else kids love. We have copies of the book here translated into many, many languages, including Braille."

Visitors to the museum also quickly learn "decoy carving is a thing," Bryce related. "Not long ago, we moved the workshop of well-known local carver Miles Hancock, known as 'Mr. Miles' to locals, onto the grounds of the museum. When it arrived, it was very clean and orderly. We were criticized by those who knew him personally. They told us his workshop was never that clean. It was always covered with wood chips and paint stains. Now that we've hosted many carvers who've made decoys in that space, it's back to its normal state. We set the calendar to November 1974, the day he died. We hope the shop looks like it did the last time he walked out of it."

An important part of the museum's mission recently is the bus tour of the Island it regularly offers during the season. "During 2021, we've been at half capacity for safety during COVID," said Bryce. "We hope to increase that next year. They're excellent. They last about 90 minutes. Experienced guides tell visitors a little about everything on the Island: history, architecture, people, and important sites. This is the first museum in my experience that's offered them."

Bryce isn't planning any sweeping changes in Museum exhibits. "I'm impressed with what we have," he told me. His chief goal now is to make sure people know it's there. Why visit the Museum of Chincoteague Island? "One young boy wrote, 'My father forced me, but I liked it,'" recounted Bryce. "It's important to get close to old things. The objects tell a story." What else should visitors to Chincoteague do? "When people ask me, 'What is there to do?' I tell them there's a whole lot to do, including the Museum, but Chincoteague is also a perfect place to do nothing at all. There's no boardwalk. No Ferris wheel.' The beach today is just as it was hundreds of years ago. Take your time. Enjoy it. Do some nothing."

RUSSELL FISH, DECOY CARVER AND BOARD MEMBER OF THE MUSEUM OF CHINCOTEAGUE ISLAND

Russell Fish never thought he'd see the day when waterfowl decoys were displayed in a museum. "I started carving in high school in the 1960s, back when they were purely for attracting birds," he notes. "I made them to use when hunting. At that time, a store would sell you a single shell if you didn't have enough for a whole box. Buying them one at a time made you a better shot, for sure."

Russell spent a Saturday in September 2021 with Crisfield's Rick Smoker, carving birds in Miles's Hancock's workshop, recently relocated to the grounds of the Museum of Chincoteague Island, where he serves on the board. "I

The workshop of Russell Fish, decoy carver.

knew Miles," he told me. "Back in the day, his decoys sold for five, maybe seven dollars. There were a whole lot of carvers on Chincoteague then. Now, only a few make a living at it. Some of us say, 'Maybe they'll be worth something when I'm dead.' The big names bring higher prices now, several hundred dollars. I do sell mine at shows. Sometimes, the cost of going to the show eats up the money you make. But it's a way to keep doing what I like to do most." Russell finds it tougher to take on a commission for a decoy. "If you're not in a hurry," he likes to say, "I'll be glad to get around to making it when I feel like it."

Russell works mainly in the old style of decoys meant for hunting. "Some purists still use wooden decoys for hunting instead of the new plastic versions. They're both good at bringing in birds. The plastic ones give you a much lighter rig. We know most of the ones we carve are going on a mantelpiece today," he admitted. "But it still feels good when someone raves about the bird you've made."

It's no easy matter to carve a decoy. "I often start with a log, from a tree. I use a chain saw first, then a band saw. That's followed by a hatchet, then a drawknife or a spokeshave." Russell explained. How long does it take? He paused a bit. "Let me think. Fifteen hours, maybe? The painting takes a while. Everyone has a little different way of carving them and painting them. Ira Hudson (perhaps the best-known Chincoteague carver) was ahead of his time. He made nicer birds. Miles Hancock worked in a more primitive style. Today, it's really more of an art form."

Russell Fish is a fifth-generation waterman. "My grandmother was born on Assateague. They moved her house to the East Side in 1917. Assateague became a federal refuge in 1943. Island. Chincoteague had electricity when she moved. Assateague had kerosene lighting. My grandfather on my mother's side served in the Coast Guard. He rescued survivors from a ship torpedoed by a U-boat off Assateague during World War II.

"I've been a commercial clammer, worked in 100, 150 feet of water on a dredger. I've led hunting parties. I've always sold decoys. It gets into your blood, into your system." Stringent regulations are making the waterman's life more and more difficult, said Russell. "Government dictates not only how many days you can work, but which days. No matter what the weather, you have to go out only on those days."

The future holds some hope for carvers. "We're encouraging young people to do it," said Russell. "They have to want to pursue something that doesn't involve a keyboard." He acknowledged the difficulty of keeping the next generation on the Island. How can they buy a home when real estate prices are soaring? "Change is for certain. But I think the current building limitations are working to keep what we have here."

"When you visit," advised Russell, "Keep that 25 MPH speed limit in mind. We appreciate it when you don't go too fast, but if you want to take a good look at something, just pull over. Some of us have places to go. Nature is abundant here. Take your time to enjoy it."

Russell understands why Pony Penning can draw 45,000 visitors. "It's our local version of homecoming," he points out. "And people from all over just love to see the ponies swimming. You might like watching them swim back two days later just as much—and that crowd is only half the size." He recommended visiting the Museum of Chincoteague Island whenever you're there. "You'll find a lot of good things in a small place," he said.

I figured a fifth-generation Chincoteaguer should know how to deal with mosquitoes. "In the old days," he advised, "When it got dark, we just went inside. After a while, you get somewhat immune to them. They do seem to like tourist blood."

Russell Fish Decoys: "word of mouth." Those who would like to own one of Russell's birds manage to find him. We're glad we did.

· CHINCOTEAGUE STEP THROUGH · TIME TOURS

Chincoteague captains conduct boat tours of all kinds, all of them waterborne. Since 2019, Cindy Faith's Chincoteague Step through Time Tours has offered visitors something different: walking tours that explore many facets of Island life, outdoors and on foot. Though Chincoteague is only about seven miles long and a mile wide, it has many stories to tell. Cindy has structured a menu of four tours that cater to individual interests.

For cultural tourists, a straightforward but fascinating walking tour puts the spotlight on local history and heroes. Cindy has genuine admiration for the leading figures that drove the Island in surprising directions over the centuries.

Beyond the history books, Chincoteague has spawned plentiful legends and lore, much of it revolving around pirates and shipwrecks. Pirates were a real presence in the area, to the delight of kids who take the tour. Shipwrecks were common; hundreds of vessels have foundered off nearby Virginia and Maryland coasts. Cindy keeps this tour family-oriented—not blood-curdling, but intriguing.

Needless to say, many visitors have a strong interest in ponies, especially those connected to pony celebrity Misty. A Chincoteague pony tour takes visitors to the Beebe Ranch, where Misty's direct descendants live, under the care of Billy Beebe.

For seafood epicures, a special Chincoteague Sampler Tour, limited to a group of ten, visits the whole town, focusing on seafood and watermen. Samples of exceptional food are served along the way. Nothing beats a full stomach for a healthy appreciation of Island culture.

Tours are held regularly throughout the day and run for about an hour and a half. Cost ranges from $15 to $45 per person (the tour, including the seafood samplers, naturally falls at the high end!) Kids under ten are free. Cindy said they often enjoy the tours more than the grown-ups.

✦ Chincoteague Step through Time Tours: (757) 894-1953
  https://www.facebook.com/
  Email: islandhistorytours@yahoo.com or cndy_fth@yahoo.com
  Chincoteague-Step-Through-Time-Tours-100169668125635

ISLAND VOICES
CINDY FAITH, CHINCOTEAGUE STEP THROUGH TIME TOURS

On Chincoteague, as in many places, people like to talk about from-heres and come-heres. "We moved to the Island when I was seven," said Cindy Faith. "That makes me a come-here." Her mother Lorraine served as director of the Museum of Chincoteague Island (then the Oyster Museum) for 25 years. Cindy and her husband moved to Governor's Island in New York City, with a view of the Statue of Liberty from their family's living-room window. Chincoteague drew her back. Nowadays, she's the Director of the Island Community House, serves on the board of the Chincoteague Cultural Alliance, is a docent for the Captain Timothy Hill House, and is a member of the Chincoteague Island Theatre Company. She started her business, Chincoteague Step through Time Tours, in

2019. Cindy plays a part in many good things on the Island.

"People are pleasantly surprised to discover how much there is to do here," she told me. "The museum has programs weekly. One hundred thirty events take place at the Chincoteague Cultural Alliance every year. The Island maintains the right balance. Visitors used to Ocean City or similar places tell me, 'This is what we were always looking for, but we didn't know it existed.'"

Cindy had 17 years of experience guiding the Road Scholar program (www.roadscholar.org) affiliated with the Museum of Chincoteague

Cindy Faith, Chincoteague Step Through Time Tours.

Island. Travelers from many nations, some intergenerational groups, come to the Island from April to November each year to learn about and explore new places.

She approached several local groups with the idea of offering walking tours to visitors. Finally, she decided to make a go of it herself in the fall of 2019.

No one imagined the impact COVID would have on tourism the next season. As it happened, Chincoteague Step through Time Tours offered exactly what cautious vacationers were seeking—a fun and educational family activity held entirely outdoors.

"It's a one-of-a-kind experience," said Cindy. "Lots of towns have walking tours, but people come here to learn about the unique history of this Island and its people. Chincoteaguers love to talk about their home. They're proud of it." By 2021, a tour schedule designed around the peak summer season had expanded to spring and fall.

For now, Cindy is handling it all herself. Next season, she may need some help. The tours have proved very popular.

Cindy Faith has a personal understanding of the magic of Chincoteague. "Let's put it this way," she told me. "When I come over the causeway, I still roll my windows down."

We get it.

▪ FESTIVALS ▪

In addition to the biggest Island event, Pony Penning, several festivals held throughout the year draw people to celebrate local culture and food. All have suffered postponements during the COVID pandemic but are expected to return when safe and practical. People miss them! It's wise to verify dates before planning around any of the festivals.

THE OYSTER FESTIVAL

The Oyster Festival, approaching its 50th year, is a one-day event held in October, the traditional return of the "oyster season." These days, you can actually eat oysters in any month of the year, even without the "R." The old saying is largely based on the problem of oysters sitting around on docks and in ships during hot weather.

The festival takes place in Tom's Cove Park, a very large and popular campground on Beebe Road. There's good local music, along with raffles and prizes ("Extravaganza!"), but the main attraction is food—some of the best seafood on this planet. You'll find clams, shrimp, oysters made multiple ways, and down-home sides like hushpuppies and fries. The festival is brief, 11 A.M. to 4 P.M., and usually sells out far in advance. The most recent ticket price was $50, which offers the festivalgoer the ultimate seafood buffet for five hours. The only additional cost: beer. How do you beat that?

My daughter and I were delighted to be in the crowd for the 2021 Oyster Festival, held after a cancellation year because of COVID. More than 2500 attended to show their joy at Oyster Woodstock. It was the biggest crowd anyone could remember. It's hard to describe the combination of Chincoteague Chill and half-hour-long lines for single-fried oysters, except to say that people go where their passion leads them. Your town's biggest church bazaar (You don't have church bazaars? Oh, my!) meets a really good local bluegrass festival. There you have it.

At Oyster Festival 2020, we met Rick from Harrisburg, Pennsylvania, waiting for oysters on the half shell. Rick's daughter brought him an IPA. He's not an IPA fan, so he gave it to me. I was grateful. These sorts of things happen at the festival.

Rick's wife began visiting the Island as a child. Now their greatest joy is watching their grandchildren playing in the ocean. "It's not like New Jersey or Delaware beach towns," Rick told me. "The island has nice restaurants, beautiful beaches, and very few bars. The town closes about 8 o'clock and doesn't open real early either. If that vibe is what you're looking for, this is the place. I've been here in late fall when the ponds were white with Snow Geese." Rick's advice to Oyster Festival guests: "Arrive early. Bring your own chairs and table. Wait until the lines die down to get the food you like. Be nice to the volunteers."

Rick knows a thing or two.

The unstoppable crew from Tom's Cove Aqua Farms steams oysters all day long. (Photos by Andrea Parmelee.)

We also met Albert Barnes, who's been shucking oysters for 55 years and can still handle 300 an hour. He was one of 15 shuckers at the tables in the big tent. They all had the technique down pat: rest the oyster on the metal spike bolted to the shucking table. Tap the hinge with a small hammer. Insert the oyster knife and flip the top shell off. Lay the shelled oyster on a paper plate. Do that six times, and the 10-year-old-girl volunteer with her hat on backward will carry it out to the waiting throng.

Albert and his colleagues did this all day. So did the oyster-fritter and clam-fritter makers, standing over tubs of hot oil. The oyster steamers (Otis, Joe, Sam, Manuel, Brian, and Marvin) kept watch on giant metal tubs propped on cinder blocks above propane burners, hauling out the milk crates full of oysters at the perfect time. Bless them all. It was a very good day.

You'll find all the stories you want to hear at the Oyster Festival. "I can't believe it's the same Island," my son told me. Me neither.

♦ Chincoteague Oyster Festival: 8128 Beebe Road, Chincoteague Island, VA 23336 (757) 336-6161 https://www.chincoteaguechamber.com/directory/chincoteague-island-oyster-festival/

Albert Barnes has been shucking oysters for 55 years. His young assistant stands ready to serve hungry customers at Oyster Festival 2021. (Photo by Andrea Parmelee.)

CHINCOTEAGUE ISLAND BLUEBERRY FESTIVAL

Chincoteague is blessed with a lovely, modern community center, Chincoteague Center (off Deep Hole Road), capable of seating 800 theater-style and well-equipped for events of all kinds. At 33 years old, the Blueberry Festival happens inside and outside the center. The blueberry harvest coincides with Pony Penning and the height of the summer beach season, so the festival has a leg up. It's held Thursday through Saturday in late July. The 2021 edition, July 22 to 24, actually happened, though Pony Penning didn't (the auction of the foals was held online, with unprecedented success). The logistics, of course, are on a very different scale. The regional artists, craftspeople, food trucks, and musicians (not to mention the blueberries) featured at the festival attract hundreds, not tens of thousands. Still, it was an encouraging turn of events for the Island calendar: "The largest fine arts and crafts event on the Eastern Shore" was back. $5 admission. How do you beat *that*?

+ Chincoteague Island Blueberry Festival: 6155 Community Drive, Chincoteague, VA 23336 Contact: Sam Serio (757) 894 2334 https://www.chincoteagueblueberryfestival.com/

CHINCOTEAGUE EASTER DECOY AND ART FESTIVAL

Over forty years old, the two-day festival celebrates the centuries-old Chincoteague legacy of decoy carving, an art originating with Native Americans that came of age in the 19th and 20th centuries. The purpose of a decoy is to lure waterfowl into shooting range. As demand grew in the 1800s for duck as an entrée, enterprising commercial hunters geared up to meet it. Along with powder and shot, they needed rafts of decoys. Carvers (often the hunters themselves), working at home with the most basic hand tools, supplied the need. Sport hunters, too, came to value their craftsmanship. The Chesapeake Bay region produced some of the nation's most prolific—and artistic—carvers. A museum at Salisbury University is named for two of the best-known, brothers Lem and Steve Ward. Notable Chincoteague carvers include Ira Hudson (among the most collectible), Delbert "Cigar" Daisey, and Miles Hancock, whose workshop now stands on the grounds of the Museum of Chincoteague Island.

Many valuable antique decoys aren't much to look at, at least to the untrained eye. They were a tool more than an art form in their day and cost very little. Modern carvers strive to please the eye while staying true to old traditions. Their creations will live on mantelpieces, not in the hulls of hunters' boats. Some carvings depict birds that aren't hunted: songbirds, shorebirds, wading birds, and raptors. Most still focus on ducks. The work of their hands is a gift in our industrial age.

For a good reason, it's called the "Decoy and Art" festival. Far more than decoys are on display: paintings, sculpture, photography, jewelry, and many kinds of woodcarving, including Easter eggs. Most are for sale. Blue ribbons are awarded in several categories.

The festival runs Friday and Saturday before Easter at the Chincoteague Combined School off Hallie Whealton Smith Drive (two Festivals were canceled because of the COVID pandemic). Five dollars gets you in. It's much tougher to get out of the building without opening your wallet if you love the region's art. Its beauty runs deep.

As you stop for the light on Main Street at the end of the causeway, the now-closed shop of local artists Hal and Helen Lott stands on your right. Hal was the creator of a long series of silkscreens honoring and promoting the Chincoteague Decoy Festival. He passed away in 2017 at the age of 97. His wife of 68 years, Claire, lives above the former shop. You can see an interview with Hal and Claire in the online archives of the Museum of Chincoteague Island.

Many of Hal Lott's posters are displayed at H & H Pharmacy. Four grace our home. They are a blessing to us.

✦ Chincoteague Easter Decoy and Art Festival: 4586 Main Street, Chincoteague Island VA 23336 (757) 336-6161
https://www.chincoteaguechamber.com/directory/easter-decoy-art-festival/

THE SEAFOOD FESTIVAL

The Seafood Festival, 50+ years old, is the spring counterpart of the fall Oyster Festival. It's held the first weekend in May in Tom's Cove Park, the large campground on Beebe Road. Just as the Oyster Festival falls a few weeks after the summer season, the Seafood Festival falls a bit ahead, perfect for early arrivals. Music, raffles, and prizes are all part of the scene, along with outstanding fish and shellfish, raw, fried, and steamed, and the traditional sides. The one-day festival runs from 11 A.M. to 4 P.M. and usually sells out. Two years have been lost to COVID; plans for 2022 are underway. It's a $50 ticket, an amazing culinary value. Don't eat for a day or so prior.

+ Chincoteague Seafood Festival: 8128 Beebe Road, Chincoteague Island, VA 23336 (757) 336-6161 https://www.chincoteaguechamber.com/directory/chincoteague-seafood-festival/

▪ THE ISLAND THEATRE AND THE ▪ CHINCOTEAGUE CULTURAL ALLIANCE

The Island Theatre was christened the Roxy when it opened in 1946—a posh name for a movie house in a small town, echoing those of big cinemas in New York and Hollywood. It's a beautiful 350-seat theatre now, carefully restored to preserve the original feel. A mix of first-run films and classics runs throughout the season. During the summer, the Chincoteague Island Arts Organization will show *Misty of Chincoteague*, filmed on the Island and the nearby Eastern Shore, which held its world premiere at the old Roxy in 1961. Misty's hoofprints, turned 90 degrees from their original angle during a sidewalk repair (no one seems certain what that angle was), remain in the cement out front. The Chincoteague Island Theatre Company also performs at the Island and at the Cultural Alliance on Church Street (the grassy lot outside is the site of the farmers and artisans market). If you're fortunate enough to be visiting when a show is running in either venue, it's well worthwhile. A good company.

+ The Island Theatre: 4074 Main Street, Chincoteague, VA 23336 (757) 336-6109 http://www.islandtheatres.com/

+ Chincoteague Island Theatre Company: Chincoteague Cultural Alliance, PO Box 257, Chincoteague, VA 23336; Center for the Arts: 6309 Church Street (757) 381-7733 Email: info@chincoteagueculturalalliance.org

ISLAND VOICES

LEXI HUBB, CHINCOTEAGUE CULTURAL ALLIANCE AND CHINCOTEAGUE ISLAND THEATRE COMPANY

"It wasn't the ponies that made me fall in love with Chincoteague," admitted Lexi Hubb, a native of York, Pennsylvania. "My parents brought me to Chincoteague camping when I was young. I remember seeing big signs warning; PONIES

KICK AND BITE. I took that to mean they were *guaranteed* to kick and bite. I wondered why anyone would go anywhere near an animal like that."

She got over it. She and her husband Justin have made their home on Chincoteague and brought new life to an Island-based theatre company. "The people created the connection between me and the Island. My parents retired to Chincoteague in 2011," Lexi recalls. I was in New York at the time, making use of my theatre degree but not finding the work I wanted. I've loved doing theatre since I was eight. A friend and I got together and proposed starting up a theatre company on the island again. Chincoteague was home to The Island Players

Lexi Hubb of the Chincoteague Cultural Alliance and the Chincoteague Island Theatre Company, creator of The Bivalve Trail podcast.

in the 1990s, but it closed when one of the founders passed away. We approached the Chincoteague Cultural Alliance at a winter retreat with the idea of reviving that. We got a green light and the donation of the existing lighting system."

The first productions were modest, hosted by a local bookstore. "It took five years for the Chincoteague Island Theatre Company to build momentum," said Lexi, "But now we're attracting more people, some with stage experience, as well as new actors." The company has performed at the CCA building on Church Street and the newly renovated Island Theatre, formerly the Roxy, built in 1945. Among its productions are original works showcasing significant events in Chincoteague Island history and the exceptional podcast *The Bivalve Trail*, created during the COVID theatre shutdown. The podcast tells the largely unknown story of Thomas Downing, a celebrated African American New York restaurateur and Oyster King of the 19th century, and the story of oystering on the Island. It's remarkably well-researched and produced—recommended listening for Chincoteague oyster-lovers and anyone about to become one.

Lexi Hubb now serves as President of the CCA. "Eighteen years ago, the CCA began with visual arts, such as the annual Plein Air Art Show. Today we host over 100 events a year, including art shows, theatre, concerts, story swaps, and the Famers and Artisans Market on the grounds of the CCA on Church Street." The market is held Wednesdays and Saturdays during the season. It has expanded recently and proved a popular outdoor event during COVID. "We're very proud of the vendors who are part of it," said Lexi. "There's so much going on here. The ponies may be the reason you want to come, but everything else the Island has to offer will bring you back."

· THE WALLOPS FLIGHT FACILITY ·

The first time we passed the huge satellite-dish farm just a few miles from the causeway, we had several theories about what it was, most pretty exotic. We weren't far off. The Wallops Flight Facility on Wallops Island has been launching rockets since before NASA was NASA: 16,000 launches at this point, some rockets as small as 10 feet long, others as impressive as the 139-foot Antares 230+ that carried four tons of cargo to the International Space Station in August 2021. Wallops is a busy place with multiple missions related to spacecraft and aircraft.

The facility began life as a World War II Naval Air Station, built in response to the sinking of two cargo ships by German U-boats just off Assateague. A teenage George H. W. Bush had a bit of fun buzzing Islanders in his fighter plane while training there. He wrote home about how locals said the word "arsters" (those Connecticut boys!). As the war ended, the age of rocketry began. NASA's predecessor established a launch site and began researching in 1945. Mercury capsules were tested there. The first payload was launched into orbit from Wallops in 1961. In the Bible of the U.S. space program, Wallops Island is part of the story from Genesis.

Though Wallops Flight Facility began during World War II, the increase in the pace of rocket launches there have made it a bigger island attraction in recent years. (Photo by Darcy and Steve Cole, DSC Photography DSCPhotography.net.)

If you're fortunate enough to be on Chincoteague when a launch is scheduled, make plans to watch. There's no need to travel to the Visitor Center viewing area on the facility's grounds. It's not much more than a couple of little-league-style bleachers, about four miles from the launch pad itself. It is the perfect spot—but wherever you happen to be on Chincoteague is pretty darn good, too, and about the same distance away from the action. To avoid disappointment, keep track online of changes in the launch schedule. NASA will often delay the launch for reasons that may not be apparent.

The beach on Assateague will close during a launch for safety. One of the reasons the facility is built next to the ocean is that a malfunctioning rocket will fall to earth over water in an unpopulated area. They don't want you to qualify as population.

The Wallops Visitor Center is definitely worthwhile for space geeks and their families, especially on a rainy day. Getting there takes only a few minutes. (Sadly, the Center has been closed through the 2020 and 2021 seasons because of the pandemic.) For those old enough to remember the "proud, happy, and thrilled" early days of the space program, it's a trip back in time. Kids, who always find a lot to like about rockets, will have a fun couple of hours in a very authentic place. There's a big story to tell about America's achievements in space flight over the last 75 years. A lot of it happened at Wallops. You'll find actual rockets on display and very cool NASA merchandise that's catching on everywhere now.

- NASA Wallops Flight Facility: Route 175, Wallops Island, VA 23337 (757) 824-1000
- NASA Wallops Visitor Center: Route 175, Wallops Island, VA 23337 (757) 824-1344; Launch Updates: (757) 824-2050 https://www.nasa.gov/centers/wallops/home

ISLAND VOICES

KEITH KOEHLER, WALLOPS FLIGHT FACILITY NEWS CHIEF

"We've been conducting research and launching rockets at Wallops Island since just after World War II," said Keith Koehler, News Chief at the facility. "Before NASA was even called NASA. But it's the larger rockets we've sent up during the last ten years, the Antares and the Minotaur, that carry satellites into orbit and payloads to the International Space Station that really get people's attention. That's what everyone loves to see."

The Wallops Island base began life as a research site for supersonic aircraft during the "Right Stuff" era of the late 1940s and 1950s when daring test pilots like Chuck Yeager began pushing the envelope of human flight. "We were a 'wind tunnel in the sky,' testing missiles and aircraft," Keith told me. "The scientific rockets came later. The waterside location close to the command center at Langley was ideal. A Naval Air Station was established on Chincoteague during the war. During the Mercury program, Wallops Island conducted research for the first human space flights, particularly on communications and re-entry. The rockets we launched here were typically smaller and sub-orbital. After their flight, they land in the water."

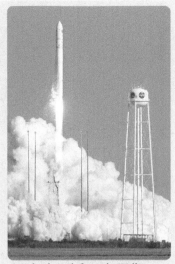

A rocket launch from the Wallops Flight Facility. (Photo courtesy of Wallops Flight Facility, NASA.)

Today's launch process at Wallops is far more complex and highly technical. "We coordinate with the FAA, general aviation, and all the recreational and commercial vessels in the nearby ocean," Keith said. "The decision to launch or delay often depends on factors someone on the ground isn't even aware of. A light rain is usually OK, but even on a windless day, the wind at 40,000 feet may be blowing at 100 mph. We monitor wind up to 100,000 feet. The small sub-orbital rockets are even more finicky than the large ones. Heavy cumulus clouds can cause a buildup of static electricity in the rocket. That's dangerous. There may be lightning too far away to see from the launch site, but if it's too close, we have to delay."

Keith wholeheartedly recommended a trip to Chincoteague to see a big launch. "That alone is worth the trip," he said. "It's a 'bucket list' experience and a great family adventure. It captures the imagination like nothing else. The night launches are spectacular. They're visible from the Carolinas, New England, parts of Canada, and as far west as Detroit. Even if you can't be here in person, we stream every launch online, with tremendous quality."

Keith himself came to Wallops Island from Louisville in 1984. Over 1800 people make their careers at Wallops Island now, most with NASA, but some with the U.S. Navy, Northrup Grumman, and NOAA, which maintains the huge satellite weather-monitoring dishes visitor pass on Route 175. "I believe the largest are about 80 feet across," Keith told me. The pace of activity at the facility should increase soon. The Antares is scheduled twice a year. The new Rocket Labs Electron should debut this year, perhaps reaching a frequency of once a month after getting underway. Wallops will surely be involved in returning to the moon, just a few years off, and Mars missions.

One of the things I like best about Assateague," said Keith, "Is that on a clear night, you can stand on the beach and see the Milky Way."

AMY BARRA, WALLOPS FLIGHT FACILITY VISITOR'S CENTER

"People stop in here all the time very confused when they see the NASA logo outside," related Amy Barra, manager of the Visitor's center on NASA's Wallops Flight Facility, just a few miles from Chincoteague on Route 175. "What are you doing here??" they ask. When they find out what we do, they're really surprised and excited." What they do, of course, is rocket science. "It's called 'rocket science' for a reason," Amy told me.

"Science on a Sphere" at the NASA Wallops Visitor Center. (Photo courtesy of Wallops Flight Facility Visitor Center, NASA.)

"'Rocket engineering' is more correct. Many people make a special trip to see the launches. We feel terrible when a launch gets delayed. I've seen people in tears over it. But delays happen for a lot of unavoidable reasons. It's like birding. You may set out one day to see a particular bird, but it just doesn't show up."

Amy knows from firsthand experience how much NASA and its mission mean to Americans. "Whenever people are asked to name good things about the United States," she said, "NASA is one of them." She was among the judges of the 2019 art competition for students celebrating the 50th anniversary of the moon landing. Entries were posted proudly on Victors' Center walls. Sales of shirts, hats, and accessories featuring the famous circular NASA "meatball" original logo and the "worm" lettering that succeeded it are booming nationwide.

Sadly, the center has been closed for two seasons by the pandemic. Amy and three full-time staff are cautiously optimistic that NASA guidelines will allow visitors again in 2022. Amy will be especially grateful for the return of "Astronomy 101" nights, a partnership with the Delmarva Space Sciences Foundation, which draws as many as 2,000 visitors at a time for a glimpse into the world of sky watching. "We start at the Bateman Center on Assateague and then move onto the beach. Amateur astronomers bring high-powered telescopes and let everyone take a look. We hold them several times a year, in-season and off-season, on both the Maryland and Virginia sides of Assateague. We enjoy scheduling them during meteor showers and other special events." Assateague is one of the darkest places on the East Coast, relatively free of the light pollution that makes stargazing difficult in urban areas.

The pandemic has also changed the role of the Victors' Center, sending its staff as "visitors" to school classrooms in 36 states on over 300 virtual field trips to teach young people about the mission of NASA and the Wallops Flight Facility. "Many of them think we're at the Kennedy Space Center on Cape Canaveral, and some of them think we're astronauts," said Amy, "But we correct that. It's an interactive presentation with activities and live chat. All our fall workshops are filled."

If you travel to Chincoteague to see a launch from Wallops, Amy advised patience. "Fewer than 200 cars fit in the parking lot for the observation area at the facility, and they fill up fast," she said. "If you have access to another good spot to view the launch, your chances are better there." The Adirondack native got used to mosquitoes and flies early but said they couldn't compare to the ones on Chincoteague. "They're less of a problem in the fall," she noted. "In many ways, the whole island is better. The water is still really warm in early fall. The crowds have thinned out. The island is beautiful when the marsh grass turns to gold. Don't hesitate to explore Route 13 up and down the Eastern Shore. You'll find many lovely little towns."

▪ THE CAPTAIN TIMOTHY HILL HOUSE ▪

Not so long ago, the lovingly restored 1800 cabin now known as the Captain Timothy Hill House looked like nothing more than a dilapidated, vine-covered old storage shed. We would routinely pass it on Main Street. Chincoteague is home to many old wooden buildings; this one was in worse shape than most. Little did we realize it was the oldest home still standing on the Island and one of the few remaining in Virginia built with a wooden chimney. That's really old—probably about 1800, though no one is entirely sure.

Restorers have done marvelous work, beginning in 2009 and culminating with relocating the structure a quarter-mile to its current location on Main Street, a short distance north of Maddox Boulevard. It opened for visitors in 2011. Extensive photo documentation on the website reveals the enormity of the job.

To step into the small sawn-plank cabin with its tiny sleeping garret is to travel back two centuries in time (what the website calls "an unexpected journey"), when the Island was a far simpler place, home to only thirty families, most of them farmers. Photos exist of older structures, but none of the buildings themselves survive.

You can tour the Captain Timothy Hill House Friday afternoons during the season and the winter by appointment. A knowledgeable docent will help you explore the house and the history of the Island with it. Be sure to ask about the sailing ships carved into the siding. It's a wonderful mystery.

- The Captain Timothy Hill House: 5122 Main Street, Chincoteague, VA 23336; Winter hours by appointment: (914) 589-7733 https://captaintimothyhillhouse.com/Home.html

▪ SHOPPING ▪

MADDOX AND MAIN STREET

Chincoteague features two main shopping areas: Main Street and Maddox Boulevard. Main Street was "downtown" back when Chincoteague first became a real town, home to the Island's first hotel and big general store. Before tourism began to boom a few decades ago, it was the business center for residents, where they'd shop for a TV, a sofa, or a Nash. Today's Main Street is home to a very different line-up: restaurants, galleries, boutiques, home décor, gourmet food, wine, coffee, antiques, collectibles, and books. It's also home to a large and lovely town park, the Chincoteague Library, and a beautifully-restored 350-seat 1946 theatre, The Island (formerly The Roxy), which shows vintage and recent films—and screens *Misty of Chincoteague* from time to time.

Main Street is a place to stroll. Find a parking spot anywhere (that may require a bit of a search some days), then take your time. There's no rush—that's the whole point.

Maddox Boulevard was named after Wyle Maddox, who arrived on the Island in 1926 as a blacksmith's helper. Though it's said he could barely read, Maddox was clearly one of those American entrepreneurs with big ideas. He started a chicken farm in the '30s and grew it into a huge operation. As the oyster industry declined (because of overfishing and an oyster parasite), many Islanders turned to chicken farming. It worked well: by the mid-50s, 5 million chickens were raised every year ("Chicken City Road" is a reminder of that era. The industry continues on the nearby Eastern shore but is gone from the Island itself). By 1950 Maddox was one of the most successful business people on Chincoteague and began developing the boulevard that bears his name. In the early 1960s, he constructed the first bridge to Assateague, a collection of steel bridge components with a wooden surface that rattled as cars drove over it. It was replaced with a far better concrete bridge when the island became a federal wildlife refuge.

We think of Maddox Boulevard as the "Main Drag." It was always the road to the beach. Until 2010, the causeway led beach traffic onto the Island by Main Street, then through downtown, then onto Maddox.

The old metal Black Narrows swing bridge is a symbol of that era. It's been gone since 2010 when the re-routed causeway began to take route traffic directly onto Maddox Boulevard. The new route makes sense in many ways, though it's understandably unpopular with the downtown merchants who were bypassed.

Though it's a two-lane road, Maddox is busy with vehicle and bike traffic. The western end has sidewalks, but it's not a place to stroll. You'll find some of everything, including many, many restaurants and food trucks, plus a farmers market-style grocer (Whiteraven's Nest). Ironically, the two big ice-cream places (Island Creamery and Mister Whippy's) are within sight of each other. There's candy, saltwater taffy and fudge, an RV repair shop, bike and scooter rentals, a bait and tackle shop, a Family Dollar, a pharmacy, a gas station, a hardware store, two miniature golf courses, and the varied kids' activities of Funland.

Major rental companies, realtors, and banks have their offices on Maddox. The local YMCA is there, too, as is the Museum of Chincoteague Island and the Chamber of Commerce. You'll find very nice gift shops, such as The Brant, where staff will make you your own "soft pony" (our granddaughter's term), similar to a build-a-bear. The T-shirt, swimsuit, and beach accessory business are thriving. Not surprisingly, McDonald's and Subway make their homes there. There's also a very nice new water park, built in 2019.

Wyle Maddox, the blacksmith, had a long-term vision. He left us in 1974, a prosperous man, but he probably wouldn't have been surprised at all by what his Boulevard has to offer visitors today.

FUN SHOPPING: BEACHWEAR, SOUVENIRS, CLOTHING, GIFTS, TAFFY, AND FUDGE

Every "beach town" is known for souvenir T-shirts. Chincoteague is no exception. Shirts, shorts, hats, towels, can cozies, refrigerator magnets, and every other kind of fun take-home item can be found in many locations, from big shops like Sunsations, Island Time, and Atlantic Shoals on Maddox Boulevard, to chic boutiques on Main Street, to unlikely spots like the Museum of Chincoteague Island and the Tom's Cove Visor's Center. My favorite Chincoteague hat, found at Tom's Cove, sports a horseshoe crab. Enjoy yourself! When your shirt says "Chincoteague," friends you haven't met yet will recognize you everywhere.

THE BRANT

A brant is a waterfowl similar to a goose, fond of a stop in Chincoteague during the fall migration. The Brant is a large and popular gift shop at Maddox Boulevard and Chicken City Road. It's a fun, pleasant place—far more than a "T-shirt shop," though you will find T-shirts, along with many other types of beachwear, footwear, giftware, foods, home décor, soaps, high-class wind chimes, a whole Christmas section, excellent stuffed toys (including the octopus, which "Doesn't make a sound," said grand-daughter) and a Build-a-Pony kiosk. We always end up at the Brant at some point and never regret it. Take your picture with Pearl the Giant Stuffed Bear on the porch.

◆ The Brant: 6472 Maddox Boulevard, Chincoteague, VA 23336
   (757) 336-5531 https://thebrantofchincoteague.com/
   Email: thebrant6472@gmail.com

ATLANTIC SHOALS SURF SHOP

You won't see surfers on Chincoteague. Skimboarders, yes, but the waves don't seem to support surfing per se. You will find a good surf shop, right on the traffic circle on Maddox Boulevard, with high-quality clothing, beachwear, sandals, and sunglasses, plus a nice selection of beer and wine. Overall, a cool place.

◆ Atlantic Shoals Surf Shop: 6758 Maddox Boulevard, Chincoteague, VA
   23336 (757) 336-1305 Email: anmkeys@yahoo.com

PONY TAILS

This iconic shop has held down its spot on Maddox Boulevard seem-ingly forever. We have only about fifteen years of history with it; many families recall much more. Our adult kids once rode the horse outside (now inside) for a quarter. We still have tiny rubber toy animals from 2005. Flattened pennies from the machine (also a quarter and perfectly legal, as the sign advised us) are in a dresser drawer . . . somewhere. Very good sweets and confections can be found at several places on the Island. Somehow, it's not a trip to Chincoteague without a stop at Pony Tales to stock up on saltwater taffy and perhaps fudge for the folks at home.

Saltwater taffy is an old confection dating to 1880s New Jersey. There's not much to it, as candies go (BTW, there's no seawater in it). The process of folding it over and over is the magic. Travelers have brought it home as a gift from the seaside for generations.

We recall watching taffy being made in an old-fashioned machine in the front of the store, back when Ralph and Lois Daisey owned it. Along with a lot of fun stuff, uniquely Pony Tails in nature, the shop carried Christian-themed giftware and books. It was a relaxing place to visit, especially with kids, who always found something fun.

The Dolle Candy Company of Ocean City, with a proud century-old history, bought the store in 2006. Some islanders didn't take that well, but the shop, and the taffy, carried on. The owners of the well-known Sunsations beachwear shop on Maddox Boulevard recently became the new owners of Pony Tails. The shop is redesigned: more modern, sleek, and Sunsations-like. The signature taffy is well-represented and still good. Fudge is on hand in many varieties. So delicious. I don't believe it has calories (right?).

♦ Pony Tails: 7011 Maddox Boulevard, Chincoteague, VA 23336
  (757) 336-6688 https://ponytailstaffy.com/
  Email: orders@ponytailstaffy.com

ART AND GALLERIES

The Islands of Chincoteague and Assateague have inspired art of every kind. How could they not? This sun-drenched world with its crown of sky and necklace of ocean and tidal marsh, home to a cornucopia of animals, birds, sea life, and colorful coastal foliage, is an artist's playground. Visual artists, craftspeople, photographers, and those unique denizens of the tidal marsh, decoy carvers, have brought the Islands to life in every art form. Their work can be found all over Chincoteague, particularly (though not exclusively) in the historic downtown, where no stroll fails to pass either a dedicated art gallery or a shop featuring local and regional art of many kinds. Ponies, birdlife, and the blue crab are well-represented. The lighthouse is a favorite subject as well. Even the marshy landscape translates well to the canvas. Craftspeople can find beauty in humble things; among our Christmas ornaments are angels made from oyster shells.

It goes without saying that art is a matter of individual taste. Visit some shops and galleries. They aren't hard to find. Browse to your heart's content. There's hardly a more pleasant way to spend time on the Islands. Find what speaks to you. Something entirely unique, conceived in the heart and made by the hands of a local artist, may be the small piece of Chincoteague that finds a place in your home.

SUNDIAL BOOKS

Really good independent bookstores are something special. The few thousand in the US are a rare treat in the digital age. One that offers new and used books and art, with a regional focus, is a real treasure. Sundial Books on Main Street, operated by Jonathan and Jane Richstein, qualifies on all counts. The store occupies a well-known corner, where the swing bridge used to end, in a bright and sunny old building once a restaurant. The central section of the ceiling between the two floors was removed decades ago, leaving a four-sided railed balcony reached by a hidden staircase. The store offers an excellent selection of books of all kinds. There's a special display of those on local subjects, along with a charming section for kids, and a curated assortment of music heavy on the Grateful Dead, usually playing on the sound system (I support this wholeheartedly). Several other rooms house an eclectic selection of secondhand books.

Regional artists are well-represented, too, visual art in particular. A little time spent browsing reveals beautiful things of all kinds. Among our family's favorites are the very modern and often gently humorous prints of Erick Sahler, "featuring the icons and institutions of the mid-Atlantic region." At home, they remind us of Chincoteague every day. You may find an artist's work that does the same for you.

✦ Sundial Books: 4065 Main Street, Chincoteague, VA 23336
   (757) 336-5825 https://www.sundialbooks.net/

a small house on the Island as a vacation place. In 2006 they heard of a local bookstore for sale. They bought it.

Friends thought they were crazy to leave salaried positions for the new venture. They forged ahead. "I'd run businesses before," said Jon, "and I was getting burned out at what I was doing,"

They began without fanfare—no ribbon-cutting or Grand Opening. Instead, they supported every Island organization they could: the Island Library, the Island Theatre restoration project, the Island Community House, and the Chincoteague Cultural Alliance. The

Jane and Jon Richstein, Sundial Books.

store sold tickets for events and served as a clearinghouse for information. They helped the Volunteer Fire Company, the police department, and the high school.

They opened the store in two small adjacent buildings but soon found a bigger and better location just a few doors down. "It's worked out well," said Jonathan. "We built the kind of bookstore we would want to go to. People meet up there to exchange information. Families tell us it's one of their first destinations on the Island." Sundial wouldn't be in business, though, without loyal resident clientele that come in year-round.

Customers remember Sundial. "We're beginning to meet folks who first came here as children and are now bringing their children. We feel like part of people's lives."

Most of the visitors to Sundial are drawn to Chincoteague by the slower pace, the chance to relax, and the environment's natural beauty. Others come mainly for the big attractions: the famous ponies, the lighthouse, and the beach. Some aren't sure what to do afterward. Jane advised a visit to the Chamber of Commerce on the Maddox Boulevard traffic circle, where 'They can tell you about everything!' "Or stop in Sundial," added Jon, "We can tell you about a few things, too. Just keep in mind it's not Ocean City."

ISLAND VOICES

ERICK SAHLER, ERICK SAHLER SERIGRAPHS CO.

Listening to Erick Sahler talk about the Eastern Shore, you just know he was born to be an artist. Artists see things in a way most people don't, even looking at the same view. God bless them for that wonderful gift. They bring beauty to the world simply by showing it to us through their eyes.

Erick is an Eastern Shore native through and through. That's also the focus of his work. "I grew up in Salisbury," he told me. "I recall clearly hearing my grandparents discuss taking the train to Philadelphia on important matters. In their day, people might go to a hospital there for surgery, or even do Christmas shopping in the big city. My Dad was a crew member on a tugboat. I joined him for a little while when I was young." If you know Erick's work, his history won't surprise you. "I worked in a T-shirt printing shop as a kid, then got my degree in Graphic Design from the U of Maryland Baltimore County, in 1989. We didn't have computers to help us yet. We created everything the old-fashioned way." He joined the staff of the Salisbury newspaper as a designer. "To my surprise, I was soon running the newsroom and became managing editor. I stayed with the paper for 22 years. For the longest time, I didn't design

Artist and printmaker Erick Sahler with some of his work.

anything. I managed people and resources. Over the years, I watched advertising revenue falling, as it did with every newspaper in the country. A change was inevitable."

In 2009 Erick bought equipment and set up a shop to create silk-screened prints. By 2011 he was operating it full-time. It's an exacting and labor-intensive process, done completely by hand, which allows an artist to create a limited number of perfect prints of an image of their creation. "Once they're gone, they're gone," Erick noted. "I wanted to create something 'counter-internet.' I use up to 14 colors. That requires 14 different screens. Each print is pulled by hand, signed, and numbered. It takes a long time—perhaps two weeks." He's recently begun to offer more modern digital reprints of some of his works. "A local hospital and the University of Salisbury wanted prints that didn't exist," he recounted. "Even I didn't know how to find one. The digital reprint makes that possible."

Erick's motto, prominent on his website, is "Eastern Shore Art for the Rest of Us," that is, for those seeking images not found elsewhere. Among the greatest challenges he faces is what to capture next. "Anything you do takes a lot of time and energy," Erick explained. "To do it, I have to fall in love with it. The problem is, I fall in love easily. I've got a long list." He captured the old Assateague Island life-saving station after seeing it in the distance. "I didn't even know it was still there. I understand a local group restored it in 2005 or so and then turned it over to the National Park Service, who have left it as they got it." He's since taken a strong interest in other old life-saving stations.

Erick creates art based in many areas on the Eastern Shore: Chincoteague and Assateague (where he finds his biggest fans, often at Sundial Books), Oxford, Lewes, Rehoboth Beach, and his hometown of Salisbury. He loves the whole area. "The Maryland side of Assateague is a joy," he said. "You can take your dog and a bottle of wine, build a bonfire, and watch the Milky Way from the beach. I love to watch Wallops Island rocket launches from a little spot called Mutton Hunk Fen in Accomack County. About 15 miles north of Cape Charles are the Savage Neck Dunes, with these fantastic sand cliffs."

In one of Erick's prints, 'Summer Sunset,' he captures the front porch of a Chincoteague cottage, with old wooden furniture seen inside. The image glows with warm light. "It's that golden hour at the end of a perfect day," he said. "In your imagination, fill in what you did that day."

I asked Erick Sahler to offer me his vision of Chincoteague. I'll let him talk without interruption. I can't improve on what he said.

"Chincoteague is a time machine. You turn off Route 13 onto 175, traveling through some hardscrabble areas that make you wonder, 'What have I gotten myself into?' Then you come upon Wallops—crazy cool with its satellite dishes. As you hit the causeway, you see Oz in the distance. A friend wrote a poem titled 'Gentle Gingoteek.' He calls that sight 'The Squint.' It's always so bright, with so much sky above. The billboards build your anticipation, one by one. Then you land at the light, and you feel yourself melt. It's so 1950s. So family.

"You leave the world at T's corner. You leave it again on the causeway. Things are still the way they used to be—and after all, 'the way they used to be' is always better."

~⌣~

Erick Sahler Serigraphs: https://www.ericksahler.com/index.html (410) 845-3774
Email: erick@ericksahler.com.

▪ SHELLS ▪

Among the things that puzzle beachgoers to Assateague is the absence of shells. On a busy beach day, the surf yields mainly broken bits and pieces—not much even worth carrying home. You're allowed a gallon of (empty) shells per person. Shell collectors assure us about a dozen varieties are available, including good-sized conchs and whelks. But where are they?

Timing is key. Everyone on the beach with you is also picking up shells—so go when you have less company, early in the morning, at the outgoing or low tide. If there's been a storm the night before, that's perfect (the winter months, when Nor'easters hit and visitors are few, are most productive). While you may hit pay dirt anywhere, you'll probably have better luck as you move farther away from heavily traveled areas. Go south beyond the parking lot towards Tom's Cove and "The Hook" at its terminus, where the Island of Assateague ends, or north towards Maryland.

Assateague is a National Seashore, its entire length open for shelling. You may want to try your luck on the Maryland side. There are only two entrances to Assateague Island: the southern, in Virginia near

Chincoteague, and the northern, near Berlin, Maryland. The border between Virginia and Maryland is only about ten miles north of the parking area in Virginia, but it takes a little driving to reach the northern entrance by road. The beach in Maryland is a state park. Much of it is a national seashore, managed by the National Park Service. You can access it by driving off Chincoteague, then taking Route 113 towards Berlin, MD. Route 611 leads to Assateague State Park—about a 45-minute trip.

Shells are available for purchase in several places on Chincoteague, often laid out on a table near the road, as with a farm stand. In a way, they are farm stands. The farm is in the surf. You pay your money and take your choice. Our favorite spot is Mary's home, near the Chincoteague High School (Home of the Ponies), on the channel side of Main Street. She has whelks and conchs for very little money, along with metal egrets.

+ Assateague Island National Seashore: 7206 National Seashore Lane, Berlin, MD 21811 (410) 641-1441 https://www.nps.gov/asis/index.htm

+ Assateague State Park (MD): 7307 Stephen Decatur Highway, Berlin, MD 21811 Campground Office and Ranger Station: (410) 641-2918 Park Headquarters: (410) 641-2020 https://dnr.maryland.gov/publiclands/Pages/eastern/assateague.aspx Email: assateague.statepark@maryland.gov Note: GPS directions may be misleading. Search for "Assateague State Park" in Maryland.

· FISHING: CHANNEL AND OFFSHORE ·

We have not gone to Chincoteague as fishermen, though we have fished in the channel, guided by local captains. We're told flounder move out of the channel fairly early in the season, leaving many other species, including croaker, an unglamorous fish that's fun to catch and good to eat if you're not looking for a lot of sport. We've cooked it. It's delicious. The captains will tell you what's running. A day on the water is a good day, whatever bites.

Visitors can fish the Assateague Channel without a license from the pier at Veteran's Memorial Park (7427 Memorial Park Drive). A saltwater license is needed for surf fishing, which can be done only outside guarded beaches and surfing zones.

Serious fishing for serious fish is a serious investment. I've never done it. If you're considering making it a part of your trip to Chincoteague, chances are you have. You've got a wide variety of choices in charters. I'll leave the decision-making to you.

+ Chincoteague.com may help you get started: https://www.chincoteague.com/charterboats.html

· CAMPFIRES AND STARGAZING ·
ON THE BEACH

Yes, you CAN build a campfire on the beach at Assateague! If the weather cooperates and it's not too warm, a gathering around a fire as the sunset melts into twilight is a memory to be treasured. Chincoteague is a relatively "dark" place, free from the light pollution of more populated areas. It's about as dark as you'll find on the East Coast without traveling to isolated areas in Pennsylvania or West Virginia (beloved of stargazers), which don't offer much other than the absence of light. On a clear night on Chincoteague, you'll see a host of stars. At times, the Milky Way is visible. You'll find photos online taken from the Island. The Milky Way is as beautiful as it is large.

If you have a self-contained metal fire pit (with a bottom—not a fire ring), you can build a fire anywhere on Assateague Beach other than the "lifeguard lanes" in front of the stations (they're marked with stakes).

Becaise it's part of the Assateague National Seashore, the beach is entirely undeveloped. Rangers and lifeguards are on duty, and facilities are good. (Photo by Darcy and Steve Cole, DSC Photography DSCPhotography.net.)

By closing time, you'll need to put the fire out (hmmm ... where to find water??), dispose of coals below the high-tide line, and carry your container out. No permit is needed. Unlike fire rings, portable metal fire pits with a sealed bottom side aren't easy to find. They tend to be large and heavy. If you've got one, go for it.

With a permit, you can build an open campfire at three areas on the beach. They're free and available from the rangers at the Tom's Cove Nature Center, on the right as you enter the parking area. The permit will indicate your site and tell you when you'll need to exit for closing time. Book your site well in advance to avoid disappointment. It's a popular family activity.

No alcohol is permitted on the beach, with or without a campfire, and your group is limited to fifty. Of course, you can't burn local vegetation or driftwood. Firewood is available in many places on Chincoteague.

♦ Tom's Cove Visitor Center (campfire permits): (757) 336-6577

▪ MAUI JACK'S WATERPARK ▪

New for 2019, right off the Maddox Boulevard traffic circle, Maui Jack's is built on part of the former Maddox Family Campground (now the Chincoteague KOA, smaller in size). Many islanders were concerned about the impact of a waterpark on the feel of the Island. To be sure, the brightly colored plastic waterslides do look out of place silhouetted against the loblolly pines, but this is a low-key waterpark if there is such a thing. It's new, clean, and fun, for young children especially. A splash zone, lazy river, and two sets of relatively low-altitude waterslides are complemented by cabanas, chaises, and a bar and grill (no Island seafood on offer here; it's typical commercial fare). Maui Jack's is open every day in-season, and prices are posted online.

♦ Maui Jack's Waterpark: 6742 Maddox Boulevard, Chincoteague Island, VA 23336 (757) 336-1800 https://www.mauijacks.com/

▪ BICYCLES AND BIKE RENTALS ▪

Is there a more ideal place to travel by bicycle than Chincoteague? The weather is lovely. The landscape is beautiful. The roads, other than Maddox Boulevard, are lightly traveled. The vehicle speed limit Island-wide is 25. There's not a hill in sight. Bicycles are commonplace everywhere: shops, restaurants, and the beach. The Wildlife Loop on the Chincoteague National Wildlife Refuge is open to bikes all the time. It's very common to see beachgoers on bikes, some with cargo (or kids) in trailers.

Some days are too warm for comfortable cycling. You're in traffic and should wear a helmet. You may not feel much of a cooling breeze. Other than that, it's good to be on a bike. Many families bring theirs. If this is your first time bringing bicycles on a trip, find yourself a bike carrier ahead of time. SUVs are the vehicle of choice for many of us, but a bit tricky to set up with a bike rack. Hitch-mounted, roof-mounted, and hatch-mounted units can work, but the choice will depend on your specific vehicle. Remember to lock the bikes onto the rack, then the rack onto your vehicle, so you don't have to watch them during stops. They can be stolen in seconds. On the Island, it's a different story.

Considering everything you'll be bringing for a beach vacation, it may be better to leave the bicycles at home (If you're a serious cyclist, consider taking a week off. With scarcely an incline on the Island, your training miles may not be all that productive). Fortunately, several places on Chincoteague rent bikes, as well as electric bikes, gas-powered scooters, and electric golf-cart-style vehicles. It's quick and easy. You'll spend $10–20 a day, depending on the type of bike and the length of the rental. You can take the bikes anywhere on the Island.

Speaking as a lifelong cyclist, I yearn for a better selection of rental bikes. Almost all are single-speed "beach cruisers." They look comfy, with wide handlebars, balloon tires, and cushy saddles. The problem is, they really aren't. Yes, you can put both feet on the ground while seated, but the saddles are too low, the bars too tall and wide, and the gears too high for comfortable riding over a distance. We'd be better off with a decent low-end mountain or commuter bike. As a former bike mechanic, I see the issue: maintenance and repair in a humid, saltwater environment. How many bike mechanics work summers on Chincoteague? Not enough. You can hose down a beach cruiser, oil the chain, and be on your way.

- ✦ The Bike Depot: 7070 Maddox Boulevard, Chincoteague, VA
  (757) 336-5511 http://www.refugebikes.com/
- ✦ Jus' Bikes: 6527 Maddox Boulevard, Chincoteague, VA 23336
  (757) 336-6700 https://www.jus-bikes.com/

+ Fun on Wheels: 6450 Maddox Boulevard, Chincoteague, VA 23336
(757) 336-5348 https://wfsites.websitecreatorprotool.com/funonwheelsci/
home.html

· KAYAKING AND CANOEING ·

If you're traveling with canoes or kayaks, you can launch from the town
dock on Main Street (near the firehouse) or boat ramps on East Side Road
or at Veterans Memorial Park (find a map on www. Chincoteague-Va.gov
under "Recreation"). You'll need a weekly ($5) or annual ($20, April to
April) boat launch permit for your vehicle, available from town offices on
Deep Hole Road or from the Police Department when offices are closed.

The folks at the Chincoteague Wildlife Refuge can show you where
to paddle for the best chance of seeing ponies, birds, and marine life.
Hand-paddled watercraft are subject to far fewer restrictions than motor-
ized craft such as jet skis and boats. At the Tom's Cove Nature Center,
Rangers offer guided kayaking tours in Tom's Cove as part of a varied
schedule of fun recreational and learning activities for families and kids.

Kayak rentals are available all over Chincoteague if you choose to
self-guide (keep in mind that the normally calm water of the channels
can get choppy and windy, just like anywhere else, and distances can be
long. Be sure your experience and fitness match the trip you're planning).

+ Big Papa SUP: 4163 Main Street, Chincoteague, VA 23336
(757) 694-8793 https://bigpapasup.com/
+ Assateague Adventures (mobile unit): 4163 Main Street, Chincoteague, VA
23336 (865) 317-2507 https://assateagueadventures.com/
+ Snug Harbor Chincoteague Kayak Tours: 756 East Side Road,
Chincoteague, VA 23336 (757) 336-6176 http://snugharborva.com/id2.
html
+ Chincoteague Island Outfitters: 7885 East Side Road, Chincoteague, VA
23336 (757) 336-5129 http://chincoteagueislandoutfitters.com/

· CLAMMING ·

You can dig for clams on Chincoteague, as residents have done for centuries. I've done it in the channel off Wildcat Cove. Tom's Cove, at low
tide, is a popular spot. No doubt there are other good places. A park

ranger or resident can advise you. You'll need a few things: a clam rake (available at Rommel's Ace Home Center); a container that floats to hold your clams; water shoes, and insect repellent. If you're clamming in shallow water, you can put your container in a swim ring. You could carry a net bag, but it's not the most convenient thing. For heaven's sake, apply a lot of bug repellent. It's best to wear a long-sleeved shirt. Move your feet, in the water shoes, along the soft bottom, digging your toes in until you feel a rock. Guess what—it's not a rock. It's a clam. Dig it up with your clam rake and put it in your basket. Bravo! You're clamming.

If you're clamming on the beach at low tide, where there's no water at all, your basket doesn't need to float. Just carry it. Scan the damp sand for a telltale 'keyhole' breathing tunnel and dig for that clam. It won't be too far down.

You can take up to 250 clams a day on Chincoteague. That's more than you have the energy to collect. By law, you can't sell them. So, eat them. That's a lot of clams.

♦ Rommel's Ace Home Center: 6735 Maddox Boulevard, Chincoteague, VA 23336 (757) 336-5808 https://www.acehardware.com/store-details/14915

▪ BIRDS ▪

ON THE REFUGE

Chincoteague and Assateague lie in a perfect spot on the Atlantic flyway for migrating birds, especially waterfowl—ducks, geese, wading birds, and shorebirds.

In times past, well into the 20th century, hunters made a living shooting ducks for the market in large quantities and shipping them north by the barrel. Today, duck is seldom on restaurant menus. Though market hunting fell outside the law, "outlaw gunners" outwitted game wardens with Island cleverness and guile, hiding their tiny boats and disappearing into the marsh after taking their quarry. One cagey hunter hollowed out his decoys and concealed the ducks inside them, then rowed home in plain sight of the law.

Before Chincoteague and Assateague became popular family destinations, the Islands were a mecca for hunters. Before the 1960s, hunters and sport fishermen made up the majority of tourist traffic, often staying at rooming houses or private homes. Duck blinds were a common sight on the Island, and the roar of guns a frequent sound in fall. Today, more visitors watch birds than stalk them.

While the Island offers birders a multitude of species year-round, the peak of the beachgoing season is not the best time to see the greatest variety. The spring and fall migration seasons are better for that. Large flocks of ducks, geese, and swans often gather in the autumn. Gulls, terns, shorebirds, raptors, pelicans, and wading birds are ever-present on the Refuge and many other places on the Islands.

21 BIRDS YOU'LL MEET ON CHINCOTEAGUE AND ASSATEAGUE

LAUGHING GULL

As the Herring Gull is to New Jersey, the Laughing Gull is to Chincoteague and Assateague. Herring Gulls live on the Islands but are vastly outnumbered by their smaller, more likable cousins. Laughing Gulls are prettier, with their ink-dipped heads, red bills and legs, and white eye-rings. Also, they laugh. It's a mocking laugh, like that kid who didn't like you laughed in the fourth grade when you tripped and dropped your lunch, but it's a laugh, nonetheless. They are less likely to steal your sandwich. If there are ten posts on your dock, laughing gulls will occupy nine by nightfall.

BLACK SKIMMER

If Groucho Marx were reincarnated as a bird, he'd be a Black Skimmer. I always picture them with cigars in their mouths. You see skimmers in two positions: standing on marshes and beaches or skimming for fish in shallow water. Skimmers are long and crescent-shaped, with a white breast and black wings and tail. They boast an amazingly long bill, also bright orange, with a black tip. The lower mandible is far longer than the upper. Standing on land, they resemble a man in a tailcoat doing a pushup. Their bright-orange legs are short and stubby. Their heads are black but only halfway down. They wear a Zorro mask.

On land, the bird is ungainly, but once airborne, it takes on a poetic grace. Its sharply pointed wings are longer than its body would require, giving it tremendous maneuverability. The skimmer maintains a controlled low-altitude flight along the water's surface, dragging its oversized lower mandible just below the surface. When it senses a fish, the lower bill snaps up as if controlled by microprocessors. The bird keeps on its flight path, perhaps zigzagging a bit, then wheels around and repeats its reconnaissance in the opposite direction. Every few passes, it lands to recover. I could watch skimmers all day. On Chincoteague in the summer, your best bet is the pools on the left of the road as you approach the beach.

TERNS

One good Tern deserves another. You'll see many lined up on the bridge to Assateague, among other places, scanning the water for fish. They take flight on amazingly long wings, then crash-land into the water to grab their meal. You'd think they'd injure themselves, but they don't. Go figure.

Watching terns is the fun part. Learning to distinguish one species from another is the tough part—a birder's nightmare. Other than size, few reliable field marks allow even seasoned birders to distinguish the several species. You could just watch them dive for fish. It's way more fun than trying to tell them apart.

BALD EAGLE

It's said that Benjamin Franklin wanted the turkey to be the national bird of the United States, but John Adams prevailed with the Bald Eagle, America's most identifiable bird. World-famous birder Roger Tory Peterson, author and illustrator of the go-to guidebook, called the Bald Eagle "all field mark," a field mark being a feature that distinguishes the bird from others.

First, it's huge, among the largest birds in the world. Birds, in general, are not large. Bald eagles are over nine pounds, with a six to seven-foot wingspan, about the same as swimming champion Michael Phelps. They're beefy and bulky. Females are a bit larger than males. When a bald Eagle reaches four to five years of age, it gets its trademark plumage: the snow-white head and tail you see in illustrations (immature birds are brown). At that point, you can't mistake it for anything else.

Once endangered nearly to extinction (a terrible fate for a national symbol), the Bald Eagle came roaring back in the final decades of the 20th century. Though protected by law since the 1940s, DDT and similar pesticides made the birds' eggs too fragile for the nesting parents to incubate. The Endangered Species Act of 1976 banned DDT and began rebuilding the eagle population.

Breeding pairs were placed in nesting sites along the East coast. The effort succeeded. Today, the sight of an eagle in the wild is no longer a

America's national symbol, the Bald Eagle, is a resident on Assateague. (Photo by Darcy and Steve Cole, DSC Photography DSCPhotography.net.)

rare treat—but still a treat. "Eagle cams" allow observers to watch nests online and see the hatching of chicks in early spring. One such cam can be viewed only in the Chincoteague Refuge Visitor Center. It's not available online, as many others are.

The nests are huge: four to ten feet in diameter, weighing tons. With luck, one to three eaglets hatch, leaving the nest in about three months.

When an eagle soars over your kayak, even its shadow tells you something special has taken place. Bald Eagles like fish, but they'll eat many things, including roadkill. An eagle diving for a large fish is a memorable sight.

OSPREY

Osprey resemble Bald Eagles if Bald Eagles had a substance-abuse problem (No offense intended, to osprey, or anyone). Like eagles, osprey are raptors, birds of prey, who pursue fish almost exclusively—ninety-nine percent of their diet. Their sharp beaks and long talons suit their hunting style. Like eagles, they're large birds with four to six-foot wingspans.

There, the resemblance ends. In contrast to the beefy eagle, the osprey has a lean and hungry look. In flight, it's athletic, swooping and diving in its search for food. Its coloration is patchy: brown and white, with black wingtips and a sort of Zorro mask on its head. Its feathers always seem in need of a good combing, whether hovering over the marsh in search of dinner or guarding its nest as you pass by on a boat. It has a stray-cat vibe. You can come very close to an osprey without startling it off its nest—but the stare you get from this very sharp, fierce bird of prey will linger.

Osprey nest very near the water, even on the water if a suitable nesting platform exists. There's only one species of osprey in the world—a rare occurrence among birds. That may be because the osprey is just so good at what it does.

PELICANS

If the Brown Pelican were a military aircraft, it would be an A-10 Warthog, the well-armed ground-attack plane beloved by pilots and ground troops despite a face only a mother could love. Watch a squad of 5 or 10 pelicans at work. You'll be amazed at their ungainly effectiveness. Their wings are broad and powerful, their wingbeats slow. They cruise above the channel or the surf at low altitude, then suddenly retract their wings and crash-land in the water, looking like they must have injured themselves. No harm done, though—a few moments later, they emerge with the targeted fish, bobbing for a few moments before re-launching for another flight. Laughing gulls make a habit of trailing after them, alert for scraps.

We think of cartoon pelicans with giant bucket-shaped bills. The extended lower section is a loose pouch of skin suspended from the bird's lower mandible. Amazingly, that pouch can hold up to 24 pounds. After a dive, most of that weight is water. Yes, its beak can hold more than its belly can (as the old limerick puts it), but the pelican can't fly with the water on board. It tips its foot-long bill sideways, emptying the pouch while holding onto a slippery fish with the hooked end.

Though its stubby legs and out-of-proportion bill make it an odd sight standing on a pier, the pelican is a remarkable bird to watch at work, either in the surf or the Chincoteague Channel.

WHITE IBIS AND GLOSSY IBIS

In ancient Egypt, the ibis was sacred. The god Thoth had the head of an ibis. Even on Chincoteague, it's a pretty cool bird. It comes in two color variations, White and Glossy. The White Ibis is snow-white, with a bright red-orange bill and legs and feet to match. It's hard to miss, wading on the

The graceful ibis, immortalized in ancient Egyptian art, wades the marsh, probing for food with its long, curved bill. (Photo by Darcy and Steve Cole, DSC Photography DSCPhotography.net.)

marsh. Its closest cousin is the Glossy Ibis, a black blob when seen from a distance, but a gorgeous blend of violet, maroon, bronze, and emerald-green up close. The best thing about ibises is their sickle-shaped, pointed bill, which they use to fish small bugs, fish, and seeds from the shallow waters of the marsh. They'll work back and forth across an area for quite a while before they take flight and relocate. They leave three-toed tracks that our two-year-old granddaughter calls "birdie footprints." Go, ibii.

MALLARD
A duck drawing in a children's book will be a Mallard: green head, yellow bill, white necklace, chestnut breast, curly tail feathers. Those are the males. Females are . . . brown. Both have little blue and white racing stripes towards the back, hard to see. We take Mallards for granted, but they're good ducks.

RUDDY DUCK
You'll spot the Ruddy Duck more quickly by its behavior than by its field marks. Granted, its markings are unmistakable: a small, round little duck with a chestnut body, white cheeks, black hood, blue bill, and sharply upturned black tail. Females are brown . . . and white. You'll know it's a

Ruddy Duck when it dives headfirst under the surface, then emerges a few feet away, bobbing like a cork. It's no wonder the Ruddy Duck can barely walk on land. They just float.

CANVASBACK

Few ducks are larger than the Canvasback, and few were more desirable during market-hunting days than the "King of All Ducks," by reputation the tastiest, because of its diet of wild celery. Over-hunting and natural challenges threatened the population as recently as the 1970s. Ducks Unlimited and the federal Duck Stamp marshaled resources for conservation. The Canvasback, a resilient bird, is hanging in there, though in smaller numbers. You'll probably suspect you're seeing one based on size alone. Strong field marks will confirm your sighting: a chestnut head and neck, black breast, white sides, and "canvas" (actually greyish brown) folded wings. Females are . . . brown but still with a sort of canvas-colored back.

NORTHERN SHOVELER

A Northern Shoveler looks like a Mallard made on a production line late on a Friday. Same duck, basically, but everything is out of place: the green head and the blue and white racing stripes are there, but the chestnut breast and the white sides are reversed. And who ordered that

(Photo by Darcy and Steve Cole, DSC Photography DSCPhotography.net.)

bill?? It's way too long. That's the Shoveler. At least the males. Females are . . . brown but still have the XXL bill.

MOCKINGBIRD

Mockingbirds are thick on the ground in Chincoteague, as in much of the American South (you should be so lucky where you live). They're lively, animated, and loud. The "mocking" part of their name indicates they can imitate the sounds of other birds (and bugs and amphibians—who knew??), which they do loudly and continuously. Mockingbirds just don't shut up or keep still. Grey, white, and black on top, the bird has an off-white breast and hops about on long legs, seemingly having a grand old time. Why not? Life is short, especially for birds.

RED-WINGED BLACKBIRD

The Redwing, the Official Bird of the Marsh, adds a "pop of color," as every designer says nowadays, to its glossy-black head-to-toe plumage and bill with a dual-striped yellow and scarlet epaulet on each wing. They are prolific singers. Their distinctive three-note tee-tee-TEE call is interspersed with little "checks" and "ticks," often while perched sideways on a reed or cattail in a marsh. They're everywhere. I don't mind that a bit.

HERONS AND EGRETS

So many tall wading birds, of so many colors and kinds! Most are herons or egrets. Most have long legs, long, snake-like necks, and spear-shaped bills. You'll see them in marshy or wet areas all over the island: ditches, marshes, ponds, and impoundments. They're also seen frequently in trees, perching above the water, sometimes in groups. Most often, they work the water alone, searching for food. Here's the rundown on who's who. All are very common:

- **Great Egret:** (Not a "great white." That's a shark.) Very large, all white, really long neck, really long yellow bill.

- **Great Blue Heron:** Very large, blue-grey, really long neck, really long yellow bill.

- **Snowy Egret:** Medium-size, all white, long neck, medium dark-colored bill, dark legs, yellow feet. (You may not see the feet, but if you do, think of an egret that stepped in highway-line paint).

This pair of buffleheads are among the many kinds of waterfowl that make the islands their home. (Photo by Darcy and Steve Cole, DSC Photography DSCPhotography.net.)

Skilled fishermen, terns crash-land in the water and emerge with a meal. (Photo by Darcy and Steve Cole, DSC Photography DSCPhotography.net.)

A Snowy Egret displays. Herons and egrets of every kind abound in the marshes and creeks. (Photo by Darcy and Steve Cole, DSC Photography DSCPhotography.net.)

- **Little Blue Heron:** Medium-size, blue-grey and reddish-grey, long neck, medium bluish bill with black tip, dark legs.

- **Immature Little Blue Heron:** Medium-size, all white, long neck, medium bluish bill with black tip, greenish legs.

- **Cattle Egret:** Medium-size, all white (fuzzy yellow crest when breeding, a little fuzzy all the time), shorter neck, shorter yellow bill, shorter yellow or pink legs. Often seen near horses.

♦ Assateague Island National Seashore Birdwatching: https://www.assateagueisland.com/birdwatching/birdwatching.htm

♦ Roger Tory Peterson Field Guides: https://www.hmhbooks.com/peterson/

THE NATIONAL SEASHORE
AND THE CHINCOTEAGUE
NATIONAL WILDLIFE REFUGE
ON ASSATEAGUE

▪ THE NATURAL ENVIRONMENT ▪

CHINCOTEAGUE CLIMATE

Chincoteague is a warm place, in summer, humid. "The winters," as Thomas Jefferson told John Adams, "are milder in Virginia." You'll find vacation rentals are often booked for Thanksgiving. While late November temperatures in Philadelphia might hover in the 40s, Chincoteague rises 10 degrees higher—quite hospitable for late fall. The island experiences high temperatures and humidity in the summer season. In a marshy coastal Southern climate, that's expected. The average high in 2020 was 77 in May, 82 in June, 88 in July and August, and 84 in September. That's pretty warm if you're accustomed to, say, New England.

The ocean warms up early compared to beaches farther north. The average water temperature doesn't fall below 68 degrees from June through October. It averages 75 in summer and can hit the mid-80s in July. That's the range swimming instructors recommend for workouts, competition, and water aerobics. You may hesitate just a bit before diving into the surf, but you'll get used to the water fast. It's refreshing but not bracing. Cape Cod, for comparison, averages 66—nearly 10 degrees cooler. The difference is noticeable. Long Beach Island, New Jersey, averages 72. If you're particular about ocean temperatures, you should be happy on Chincoteague. It's not Miami Beach (summer average, 84 degrees), but not too far off.

MOSQUITOES AND FLIES

Mosquitoes and biting flies are simply part of the Island ecosystem, so much so that many souvenir items feature them (my collection includes a shot glass with a cartoon mosquito and the slogan, "Send More Tourists!"). The mosquito, say locals, should be the State Bird. Biting flies (small black critters) are perhaps even worse. Their tiny, scissor-like jaws create an incision to draw blood. You'll feel it. Swatting them and flailing your arms probably attracts more, or so we hear.

Repellent or protective clothing is an absolute necessity. Your repellent should include high concentrations of DEET or Picardin. If you choose a natural or non-chemical alternative, look for oils of lemon eucalyptus, peppermint, lemongrass, cedar, rosemary, and clove, used in brands such as Murphy's Naturals, Herbal Armor, No-Bite-Me, Buggins, and Badger. We've used several. Whatever their effectiveness, they smell great—a real plus! What works against mosquitoes doesn't necessarily work against flies, which are tougher customers. Experimentation is your best bet. Some swear by Avon Skin-so-Soft, an old product not developed for use as a bug repellent but quite effective, according to its devotees. Johnson's Baby Cream with Aloe is another off-label alternative some folks advocate.

Anti-mosquito measures used by the town of Chincoteague include truck-mounted mobile foggers and a plane that tends to arrive early in the morning. Its vintage rotary engines are music to the ears of Chincoteaguers, who like to post online "The plane! The plane!" (It's been decades since Ricardo Montalban and Herve Villechaize starred in *Fantasy Island*, but the phrase endures on Chincoteague.) The town website describes measures being taken: https://chincoteague-va.gov/mosquito-control/

At the beach, wind from the east blows bugs onshore into the marsh. Wind from the west blows them towards beachgoers. If there's no breeze, bugs will find their way to you. When that happens, most people choose to leave and return at a better time. Mosquitoes and biting flies are active May through November, when frost will eliminate them . . . until next year.

Don't let bugs keep you from Chincoteague. Do take measures to protect yourself, including protective clothing, if you plan to spend time in wooded areas of Assateague and the Chincoteague Island Wildlife Refuge. Be ready to adjust your plans if bugs are biting badly. You'll know soon enough. Residents and frequent visitors enjoy complaining about the mosquitoes, comparing notes on dealing with them, and venting about how bad they are on a particular day. Still, residents don't move away, and frequent visitors don't stop visiting. We wouldn't dream of letting a few (or quite a few) bugs come between us and the island we love.

We don't even mind the novelty t-shirts. Our favorite is one we saw an older gentleman wearing in The Brant gift shop. It was plain white and well-worn, with "Chincoteague" in navy blue on the top line, then a navy-blue mosquito, then "Island" in the same color on the bottom line. That's all. A true classic. He couldn't recall where he got it, only that it was "some years ago." You could make a town flag out of it. We can only imagine the conversations at the Chincoteague Chamber of Commerce:

"We're going very big on the mosquito souvenirs this season. The tourists can't get enough of them."

"George, can we please stop placing such an emphasis on the *mosquitoes?*"

"I don't know, Fred. The mosquito-themed stuff does really well for us."

· THE NATIONAL SEASHORE: ·
NON-COMMERCIAL . . . WITH PARKING!

If you're planning your first visit to Chincoteague and are accustomed to a Long Beach Island/Ocean City/Rehoboth Beach/Cape Cod/Long Island scenario, prepare yourself for an almost unbelievably pleasant surprise: the beach on Assateague is completely accessible. There is no development. None. No homes, hotels, or condos. Not even a hot-dog stand. No structures stand on the beach except lifeguard stations, changing rooms, and a few environmentally friendly toilets (ingenious and relatively pleasant). The federal government doesn't do everything well (don't get me started), but it maintains the Chincoteague National Wildlife Refuge, and its beach, very well. Here's what you do: drive or cycle a few pleasant miles from the town of Chincoteague along a paved access road. Pay a very reasonable access fee ($10/day, $25/week, $45/year, $80 lifetime for seniors), turn left or right at the Tom's Cove Nature Center. Find a parking spot (the 1000-vehicle lot can fill up on a busy day, but we've done well). Unload your gear. Walk a few dozen yards onto the beach. You're golden. *Can you believe this?*

Long-time residents remember the old beach fondly. Years ago, it was a roomier place, with dunes and wooden fences protecting them. Natural forces (some say man-made structures farther north) have changed the shape of this beloved piece of Virginia seashore. Storms and tides have altered the map of Assateague, Tom's Cove, and "the hook" at its terminus. Federal resources have been deployed to preserve a favorite destination of millions. "Overwash," a storm surge that carries seawater past the beach into inland coves, has caused engineers to question the long-term viability of the beach and parking area as it stands. Proposals were made to move the parking area some distance away and shuttle visitors to the beach. The reaction was negative. Nothing compares to the joy of parking fifty yards from the surf.

The lot is constructed of sand and shells. At times, storms have their way with it. It may be full of serious potholes, temporarily. Go slow (a little taste of off-roading in your Subaru). The faithful crew will soon be out at sunrise with front-end loaders, making it right again. They've got your back. You don't have much ground clearance, especially with the Yakima rooftop carrier loaded with boogie boards, dune spoons, a sun shelter, a cooler, and a collapsible beach wagon.

Sand wheelchairs are available on Assateague at no charge. Arrangements can be made through the Tom's Cove Visitor's Center. It's a bit tricky. They're kept in storage sheds off the parking lot (last we checked, there were two), and the keys are kept at the Visitor Center. You reserve the wheelchair, use it to get to the beach, and return it when your stay is over. During that time, it's "in use." If someone hasn't returned it on time, the next person may face a wait.

The wheelchairs are fine on the portable walkways provided in a few areas for the first stretch of the walk but soon bog down on actual sand. You'll need a strong person to propel one.

What does the future hold for the beach at Assateague? It's fair to say no one knows, even professionals whose mission is to predict such things. Its geography has changed even in the limited time we've kept track, let alone over its long geological history. The lighthouse was moved long before people dedicated themselves to preserving the landscape. In the two decades we've been visiting that small stretch of sand, it has narrowed, then deepened again. In the face of powerful forces (the moon controls the tides, after all), my best advice is to enjoy a beach as it is right now, as easily enjoyed as any beach in history. Go.

Our favorite seaside lunch is Mediterranean Tabbouleh Wraps from the Sea Star on Maddox Boulevard. Bring your favorite lunch, along with your boogie boards, dune spoons, sun shelter, and beach wagon. Have a seat. Listen to the surf or play in it. Take a nap. You could use one, right? Life's good.

♦ Chincoteague National Wildlife Refuge: 8231 Beach Road, Chincoteague, VA 23336 (757) 336-6122 https://www.fws.gov/refuge/Chincoteague/

BAYSIDE: TODDLERS

Across the parking area from the surf side of Assateague Beach, those with toddlers will find a precious, even vacation-saving resource: Toddler Beach. That's not its official name—it doesn't even have an official name. The lovely little oval body of seawater between the parking lot and the Tom's Cove Nature Center is the perfect spot to take your little one who can't yet deal with the waves. Set up your beach chair and cooler, dig in the sand and mud, and swim. Maybe take the one-year-old for a splash— certainly the two-year-old. They won't have to deal with the rollers. At low tide, there isn't much water. You won't enjoy the experience as much. At high tide, you're fine. A little ways out, it's a muddy bottom, with grass and weeds. The tide covers that. It's a very relaxing day. No lifeguard on this side. No riptides, either. You'll see birds working in the area. The breeze is lighter. You'll feel a bit warmer. When the wind is from the west, it blows flies in your direction—but that's also true of the actual beach. This is your spot, moms and dads of little ones in swim diapers!

TOM'S COVE VISITOR CENTER

When you're done for the day—or before you begin—visit the Tom's Cover Visor Center, at the turn into the parking area. It's open daily from 9 A.M. to 5 P.M., April through November, with limited winter hours. It's a fun, quick stop, especially for small children. Very helpful rangers will assist if needed, but it's quite manageable. A large saltwater aquarium features small fishes, crustaceans, and snails native to the Island. A 6' square touch tank (closed in 2021 because hand sanitizer was intolerable to the creatures) features more Island marine life. Nearby, you can handle whale vertebrae, a dolphin skull, and more ocean-related objects.

The souvenirs and books here are real (though not all made in the USA, as National Park merchandise should rightly be): adorable soft ponies, Assateague ball caps adorned with horseshoe crabs, even rubber horseshoe crabs with moveable pincers. Pull into the parking lot in front or hike a bit from the Toddler Beach area on a sturdy boardwalk for a cool little adventure. You'll find online a schedule of wonderful events the rangers conduct for kids, including kayaking in Tom's Cove, searching for marine life in the surf, birdwatching, and a whole activity based around the blue crab. This is a fun way for kids to get to know the Island with the guidance of real experts. Insect repellent. INSECT REPELLENT!

✦ Tom's Cove Visitor Center, 8586 Beach Road, Chincoteague, VA 23336 (757) 336-6577 https://home.nps.gov/asis/planyourvisit/hours.htm

THE H.H. BATEMAN VISITOR CENTER

The H. H. Bateman Visitor Center at the Chincoteague National Wildlife Refuge is delightful. It's a well-designed, low-key respite staffed by professionals, where adults and kids can learn a lot in a truly enjoyable way—about eagles, shorebirds, marine life, and the marvelous wildness around you. Life-size dioramas await, while a first-class auditorium hosts talks by knowledgeable people about the natural world. The Center serves as the hub for several trails. Rangers can share the schedule for foot and bicycle traffic and vehicles. A drive around pools and fields maintained by the refuge will often yield a good assortment of birds. Among the charms of the Visitor Center are old-fashioned wooden rocking chairs on its veranda. They communicate the stress-free nature of the place from the moment you step onto the porch. Stop in. It's worth a visit.

H. H. Bateman, in case you're wondering, was a lawyer and Air Force Veteran (Korea) educated at William and Mary (Jefferson's alma mater) and Georgetown. He served in the Virginia Senate and U.S. House for 32 years. Originally a Democrat, he ran as a Republican after 1976. Bateman was a popular guy. He won his closest election by ten points. He died on the golf course in 2000. His son is the mayor of Newport News, Virginia.

✦ Chincoteague National Wildlife Refuge, 8231 Beach Road, Chincoteague Island, VA 23336 (757)-336-6122
https://www.fws.gov/refuge/Chincoteague/

Ducks on the wing over the wildness that is Assateague. (Photo by Darcy and Steve Cole, DSC Photography DSCPhotography.net.)

ALCOHOL-FREE ENVIRONMENT

You won't find throngs of partiers on Assateague. Throngs, yes—it's a really popular beach—but no partiers. Coolers abound, but none carry alcohol, at least according to law. Alcohol is prohibited on Assateague, in the State Park in Maryland, and the Chincoteague National Wildlife Refuge. We haven't seen any effort to check—but those are the rules. If your perfect evening includes a sunset toast with a bottle of bubbly, you're out of luck (and I'm sorry to miss the occasion). The trade-off is a peaceful and serene family environment on the beach. Save your cocktails for the porch or deck and enjoy a beach where the loudest noises are the roar of the surf, the laughter of omnipresent gulls, and the squeals of children racing the waves. The beach is clean, safe, and well-supervised by the lifeguards and rangers of the Department of the Interior. Bless them for their good work.

PARK RANGERS

When our youngest child was six, he got lost on the beach. Some of us were swimming, some looking in another direction, when he took it upon himself to wander off. His little shoes were there on the beach towel, but no matter where we looked, we couldn't see him. My daughter, 16 then,

A summer rainstorm passes, leaving a double blessing on the marsh. (Photo by Darcy and Steve Cole, DSC Photography DSCPhotography.net.)

later admitted she feared momentarily he might have run into the ocean and been carried away, and his shoes were all that were left. That occurred to me, too. These are the thoughts that creep into your mind when a little one is missing on a crowded beach. We quickly split up, phones in hand, to search in all directions. In about ten minutes, we got a call from a park ranger. They had him in custody. He chased off after something—no one remembers what—then couldn't locate us. He searched for a ranger until he found one. Two, in fact, were very official in full uniform when they delivered him. He remembered all our phone numbers. They dialed until someone answered. That little boy is a volunteer firefighter now. He comes to the Island with us every year. Good people, those Assateague park rangers. We still owe you one. If you're reading this, thank you.

· DOGS ·

Your dog is welcome on Chincoteague Island and in the town of Chincoteague. Stores and restaurants set their own policies on bringing dogs inside. Hotels and rentals are also clear on their pet policies. Some allow pets; most don't. If bringing your pet is a priority, it won't be too difficult to narrow your search for accommodations right from the start with a call or an email. While many vacationers choose to board their animals

A band of wild ponies graze in the shadow of the lighthouse on the refuge on Assateague. (Photo by Darcy and Steve Cole, DSC Photography DSCPhotography.net.)

near their homes, pet boarding services are available on or near the Island. You'll want to do your own research to ensure the particular service offers what you're seeking. Pets are family!

A dog park has been open to the public since 2019 with an annual permit ($35) or a weekly permit ($15) you can get at the town office on Community Drive. The park is on Hallie Whealton Smith Drive across from the entrance to the Island Nature Trail. It's divided into sections for larger and smaller dogs, equipped with doggie-waste bags and watering bowls. Your well-behaved pup can run off-leash with you and its leash nearby. We've never seen it busy.

Assateague is an entirely different story. Except for service dogs, no pets are allowed in the Chincoteague National Wildlife Refuge on Assateague Island. This applies to the entire Virginia portion of Assateague. Please allow me to repeat that: NO PETS ARE ALLOWED ON ASSATEAGUE ISLAND IN VIRGINIA. You may not bring them to the beach. You may not walk them on the trails. YOU MAY NOT EVEN HAVE PETS IN YOUR VEHICLE. It's U.S. Fish and Wildlife Service policy. The justification offered is, "To protect wildlife, habitat, and visitors." Signs are posted as you cross the bridge from Chincoteague to enter the refuge, but many of us aren't paying close attention to signs while on vacation.

A duck blind in the channel testifies to the Island's legacy of hunting and decoy carving. (Photo by Darcy and Steve Cole, DSC Photography DSCPhotography.net.)

You may ask how it can harm "wildlife, habitat, and visitors" to have your dog in your car. It can't, of course. Refuge administrators are looking at the potential chain of events. Sooner or later, it's likely that someone with a dog in their car will need to let the dog out. Next thing you know, the dog is chasing an adorable Delmarva Fox Squirrel, only recently recovered from endangered status.

Some people are wonderful about minding rules. Some just aren't. You may have seen a video of visitors to Yellowstone trying to pet a one-ton bison or Eastern beachgoers harassing an 800-pound pony. Things can go bad quickly. Putting on the ranger's hat for a moment and considering the impact of 1.5 million visits a year to a relatively small piece of land, a policy that seems too strict may begin to make sense.

Service dogs, "as defined by the ADA," are permitted in the refuge on a six-foot or shorter leash. Rangers will assume that a "service dog" would be doing its job, not running loose.

♦ Town of Chincoteague Dog Park, Hallie Whealton Smith Drive
   https://chincoteague-va.gov/skate-park-rules/ (The address is mislabeled but correct)

· TRASH ON THE BEACH ·

We've seen very little trash on the beach over the years. Occasionally, some folks (who just weren't raised right) leave stuff behind. It's a great idea to take along a plastic supermarket bag and pack that out. Seabirds eat it. It can do serious harm. Thank you!

A GOOGLE MAPS ERROR

As of 2021, Google Maps indicates that a drivable road links the Virginia and Maryland beaches on Assateague, off Wildlife Drive. No such road exists. The only way to access the Maryland side of Assateague Island is to drive west off Chincoteague over the causeway and take public roads to Assateague State Park in Maryland. No doubt Refuge officials are working on the problem with Google. Ever tried to contact a large tech company to solve a problem?

WHERE TO STAY

▪ NATIONAL CHAINS ▪

Hampton Inn and Suites, Comfort Suites, Best Western, Days Inn by Wyndham, and Fairfield Inn and Suites operate busy hotels in very good locations on the Island. Reviews are plentiful on popular travel sites. If your plans include a traditional hotel, you shouldn't have difficulty finding one that works. The Best Western, Days Inn, and America's Best Value Inn are on Maddox Boulevard, which carries the most traffic on the Island. The other three national chains are built on the Chincoteague Channel facing west, meaning that if you have a channel-side room, the sunset comes as a bonus. Not all rooms offer that view, but some hotels set up welcoming lounge chairs for guests who seek the daily nirvana of the setting sun. Ask about that if you are a sunset fan (you are—trust me). The recently built Marina Bay Hotel and Suites, also on the channel, is not part of a chain per se but is part of the Ascend Collection of hotels, an alliance of independent properties who have banded together for greater success in a chain-hotel landscape.

The only chain hotel we've stayed at on the Island is the Hampton, and that only briefly. Each year their sign on Main Street boasts of their status as the number one or number two-ranked hotel nationwide in the huge Hampton group. That's no easy task. A display case in the lobby houses serious national awards for excellence. Hampton Inns and affiliates in the Hilton family are my go-to for business travel. If you're part of a hotel rewards program with a property on Chincoteague, what better way to use your points?

♦ Hampton Inn: 4179 Main Street, Chincoteague, VA 23336
   (757) 336-1616 https://www.hilton.com/en/hotels/ccgvahx-hampton-suites-chincoteague-waterfront/ Email: info@chincoteaguechamber.com

- Fairfield Inn: 3913 Main Street, Chincoteague, VA 23336 (757) 336-0043 https://fairfieldchincoteague.com/ Email: info@fairfieldchincoteague.com

- Comfort Suites Bayfront Resort: 4195 Main Street, Chincoteague, VA 23336 (757) 336-3700 https://www.chincoteaguecomfortsuites.com/ Email: gm.va067@choicehotels.com

- Best Western: 7105 Maddox Boulevard, Chincoteague, VA 23336 (757) 336-6557 https://www.chincoteague-hotel.com/ Email: info@chincoteague-hotel.com

- Days Inn by Wyndham: 7020 Maddox Boulevard, Chincoteague, VA 23336 (757) 828-4835 https://www.hilton.com/en/hotels/ccgvahx-hampton-suites-chincoteague-waterfront/ Email: daysinnontheisland@gmail.com

▪ LOCAL HOTELS, INNS, AND ▪ BED-AND-BREAKFASTS

As for local hotels, motels, inns, and bed-and-breakfasts, choices abound.

LOCAL HOTELS

Any community where tourism is the primary industry offers a wide variety of local hotels and motels. At least ten, some quite large, operate on the Island, most on busy Maddox Boulevard or Main Street, on the channel, plus several "cottage" operations that offer stays in a separate building not much bigger than a hotel room or suite. Generally, they're built around the old-fashioned exterior-entrance layout beachgoers may remember from previous decades. Many have a retro or "mid-century" feel because they were built in the 1960s when "guest houses" on the Island yielded to the modern multi-unit motels tourists had come to prefer. Others are more recent. The Sea Shell Motel, one of the more picturesque, is tucked away in a residential area about a block off Main Street. It dates to 1965. A few of its original units were constructed as housing for World War II soldiers stationed on the Island. It offers cottages of all sizes, in addition to rooms. The older places have undergone many renovations and updates in decades since, but their foundations were laid when the NASA crew at Wallops Island across the channel was launching some of the first satellites into space.

Because our family is a larger group, we've gravitated to rental homes during trips to Chincoteague. We haven't experienced local hotels first-hand. Many travelers have. You'll find plain-spoken reviews all over the

Internet. The price point is a major attraction of many of these long-established hotels. Family ownership and personal service are others. They include The Anchor Inn, The Atlantic Shore Inn, The Chincoteague Inn, Holiday Cottages, The Island Motor Inn Resort, The Lighthouse Inn, The Refuge Inn, The Sea Hawk Motel, the Sea Shell Motel, Snug Harbor Cottages, and The Waterside Inn. I may have overlooked others. My apologies to them.

+ The Anchor Inn: 3791 South Main Street, Chincoteague, VA 23336 (757) 446-6313 https://www.chincoteague.com/anchor/ Email: anchorinnofc@verizon.net

+ The Atlantic Shore Inn: 6273 Maddox Boulevard, Chincoteague, VA 23336 (757) 336-6565

+ The Chincoteague Inn Motel: 4417 Deep Hole Road, Chincoteague, VA 23336 (757) 336-6415 https://www.chincoteagueinnmotel.com/ Email: chincoteague@comcast.net

+ Holiday Cottages: 6113 Taylor Street, Chincoteague, VA 23336 (757) 336-6256 https://www.holidaycottageschinco.com/ Email: holidaycottageschinco@gmail.com

+ The Island Motor Inn Resort: 4391 Main Street, Chincoteague, VA 23336 (757) 336-3141 https://www.islandresortinn.com/ Email: reservations@islandresortinn.com

+ The Lighthouse Inn: 4218 Main Street, Chincoteague, VA 23336 (757) 336-5091 https://www.mylighthouseinn.com/ Email: info@mylighthouseinn.com

+ The Refuge Inn: 7058 Maddox Boulevard, Chincoteague, VA 23336 (757) 336-5511 https://www.refugeinn.com Email: refugeinn@verizon.net

+ The Sea Hawk Motel: 6250 Maddox Boulevard, Chincoteague, VA 23336 (757) 336-6527 https://seahawkchincoteague.com/ Email: seahawkmotel@verizon.net

+ The Sea Shell Motel: 3720 Willow Street, Chincoteague, VA 23336 (757) 336-6589 https://seashellmotel.org/ Email: info@seashellmotel.org

+ Snug Harbor Cottages: 7536 East Side Road, Chincoteague, VA 23336 (757) 336-6176 http://snugharborva.com/ Email: snugharbor@verizon.net

+ The Waterside Inn: 3761 South Main Street, Chincoteague, VA 23336 (757) 336-3434 https://watersideinn.biz/ Email: donna@watersidemotorinn.com

LOCAL INNS AND BED-AND-BREAKFASTS

Bed-and-breakfasts carve out a place in the hospitality world by offering travelers something rare in the modern era: charm. Conventional hotels are trending towards Euro-style sleekness, where charm is in short supply. You don't choose a bed-and-breakfast for roominess or modernity, but instead for a unique mix of traditional furnishings, pleasant common space, beautiful grounds, carefully chosen food, and a level of capable personal service unavailable elsewhere. The typical bed-and-breakfast is a large, luxurious private home from a bygone era. Each room has its own appeal. Chincoteague and the nearby Eastern Shore are home to several. Three on the Island stand within shouting distance of one another downtown.

I can't offer reviews, but I can offer some perspective on how they fit into the lodging picture on the Island. Past guests have posted many reviews on popular sites that will prove helpful in choosing which suits your travel style.

Websites are heavy on pictures and video, a good choice for a property that trades on quaintness and charm. You'll see lovely photos of high tea, cheese and charcuterie boards, private gardens, large sitting porches, and chess boards set up in front of a fireplace. The adjective "cozy" gets a good workout. Antique furnishings predominate. Loaner beach gear and binoculars are favorite perks. Travelers often return because of the personal service of the hosts. They know the Island and serve as local guides. Properties change hands from time to time, with a corresponding change in direction. Return guests will often mention that.

Perhaps the best-known is Miss Molly's Inn, a large, traditional bed-and-breakfast on Main Street downtown where Marguerite Henry stayed in 1946 to write *Misty of Chincoteague*, the children's book that put the Island on the map. You can stay in her room if you like. You'll find the big brass beds, lace curtains, and striped wallpaper reminiscent of another era.

The Channel Bass Inn, long an anchor of the corner of Main and Church Streets, also occupies an old Island building, constructed in 1892 and converted for lodgers in 1920. It's known for its beautiful and tranquil Southern garden.

The Watson Guest House, with its gingerbread-festooned sitting porch, could have time-traveled from the era of Mark Twain.

The Island Manor House also began life in the 19th century as a single T-shaped structure, the residence of a doctor and the Island's postmaster. In a fun plot twist, the two men married sisters. The house was split in two to create separate residences for the couples, then re-connected by the addition of a sunroom when converted to an inn in the 1980s.

If you gravitate towards bed-and-breakfast-style accommodations, plan well ahead. Inns on Chincoteague boast fewer than ten rooms and are booked far in advance at peak times. Many travelers treasure the experience and look forward to returning.

- Miss Molly's Inn: 4141 Main Street, Chincoteague, VA 23336
  (757) 336-6686 https://missmollys-inn.com/
  Email: hosts@missmollys-inn.com

- The Channel Bass Inn: 6228 Church Street, Chincoteague, VA 23336
  (757) 336-6148 https://www.channelbassinn.com/
  Email: innkeepers@channelbassinn.com

- The Watson Guest House: 4240 Main Street, Chincoteague, VA 23336
  (757) 336-1564 https://www.chincoteague.com/watsonhouse/
  Email: relax2477@aol.com

- The Island Manor House: 41600 Main Street, Chincoteague, VA 23336
  (757) 336-5436 https://islandmanor.com/
  Email: islandmanorchincoteague@gmail.com

▪ THE RENTAL PICTURE ▪

Renting a home, large or small, is a popular option for families or larger groups planning a stay on Chincoteague: so popular that a half-dozen agencies (some also realtors) make it their business. Depending on the season, rentals are available by the day or week, with minimum stays applying during the summer. Many agencies post a chart of rates and availability for each property; if there's one that strikes your fancy and suits your schedule and budget, you may end up making plans with that home in mind.

Be careful with listings stating how many people the property "sleeps." That number may include a sofa-bed in a common area. Many rentals have one. Bunk beds are also popular.

Naturally, rates vary with the calendar. You'll often find off-season, mid-season, and "peak" season pricing, along with a premium rate for Pony

Penning Week. Chincoteague in the off-season is a travel bargain. Many people with flexible schedules prefer to visit after summer has passed. Fall weather is lovely. The trade-off is that many restaurants operate on limited schedules or close altogether when the number of visitors falls.

A wide variety of homes are available as vacation rentals. The traditional Island home is known popularly as a "waterman's cottage:" a small wood-framed two-story house built close to the street. These were the humble residences of fisherman, oyster tongers, and crabbers of the not-so-distant past when seafood was king on Chincoteague.

Though some still serve as primary homes, many have been remodeled and updated for the rental market. They line the pleasant, lightly traveled streets of downtown neighborhoods and the east side of Main Street south of town, where many enjoy a good view of the channel with its sunsets. We've stayed in several. They are a fine choice for families. Expect steep stairs, upstairs bedrooms on the smaller side, and traditional bathrooms, unless the new owner has gone full-bore with a remodel. Kitchens have generally been updated to serve the needs of enthusiastic home cooks. Well-renovated cottages are often bright, airy, and comfortable. Screened porches are a welcome bonus (an unscreened porch, however attractive, tends to be far less useful on the Island, where mosquitoes can be a big issue).

Even smaller, older properties, when re-done well, command a premium price in Chincoteague. As I write this, one such home is listed for nearly $400,000, a price that would astonish the original builder. It's common practice for homeowners to stay on the Island a few weeks a year and list with one of the rental agencies for the rest. You'll often see Thanksgiving blocked out on online calendars. What better place to celebrate that joyful family holiday?

Far more modern homes are also on the rental menu, some built recently, as the Island's reputation has spread. (You'll see many properties under construction during your visit). They range in size from modest to extravagant. Some feature five or more bedrooms, great rooms for family gatherings, and expansive kitchens, while others are typical ranch-style or two-story homes. Condo-style units in multi-story buildings (three stories max—this isn't Ocean City), particularly on the bay on the southeast side of the island, are easy to find for rent.

As you travel north on Main Street, you find homes built on the west side of Main, directly on the channel, often with a pier for channel access. This game-changer allows crabbing, kayaking, birding, or sunset-watching waterside. The typical dock is four feet wide and many, many feet long. Between the homesite and the actual channel lies a long stretch of tidal marsh, with tall grasses, tiny fiddler crabs, turtles, and egrets. Owners of homes in such lucky spots usually build as much glass as possible into the side facing the setting sun.

PLANNING FOR A RENTAL

The advantages of a rental are many: square footage, privacy for family or group members, common space for gatherings, a comfortable retreat during bad weather, and a kitchen to enjoy takeout, home cooking, or grilling (not on the porch or deck—that's illegal). Hey—Moms and Dads: washer and dryer *right there!* Yes, you need to pack sheets and towels (or rent them—a convenient option, not too pricey), but you'll get away with fewer changes of clothes, let alone beach towels. Piers, docks, porches, and gazebos are a big plus. A rental suited to your group is a fine place to relax on an Island tailor-made for relaxation. A rainy day, or one when everyone is low on energy, isn't necessarily a bad day when you can hang out together. Coloring? Puzzles? (Even TV?)

The disadvantages are only two: you may, depending on the size of your group, spend more per night, and no staff will be on duty.

When planning for a trip to a rental property, keep in mind the need to care for a house for the length of your stay. Not emergencies and repairs, of course. If something unanticipated happens, rental agencies are on call and will come to your aid. Capable people can be dispatched quickly to fix a malfunctioning A/C unit or appliance. The few issues we've had over many years were attended to speedily. When a toaster gave up the ghost, the rental agency handed me a $10 bill and sent me to Family Dollar. Problem solved.

Routine care is up to you: cleanup, kitchen chores, and laundry, as it is at home. In a rental, you can't forget about daily housekeeping altogether. For some folks, that's a deal-breaker (It's such a relief to return to a perfectly clean hotel room at the end of a busy day). For others, it's a good trade-off.

Your rental will be spotlessly clean when you arrive. That's been our experience, with many different rentals from two agencies. It's been reassuring during the two visits we made to Chincoteague during the

"COVID years" of 2020 and 2021. Your agency will ask that you leave your rental in good condition: nothing left behind (especially food), trash out, counters cleaned, floor swept, and refrigerator wiped down inside. The cleaning crew will take care of the rest.

When you arrive, there won't be food of any kind. There may be leftover supplies such as trash bags and dish and laundry soap, but you'll need more. If you're blessed with space in your vehicle, bring household necessities, along with staples like coffee, tea, and sugar. If space is tight (welcome to the club!), make your first supply run to Island Foods on Cleveland Street (a short drive), one of the two dollar stores on the Island, or back off-island twenty or thirty minutes to Food Lion in Oak Hall or Walmart in Pocomoke, the closest larger stores.

It's a pastime among Chincoteaguers to point out the shortcomings of Island Foods, the town's only supermarket. It's very small, like supermarkets decades ago, but you'll likely find what you need. The selection is more limited than back home. The prices may be a little higher, too. They have store brands in most categories. I'm OK with Island Foods—and I shop at Wegman's, the best supermarket imaginable. You'll probably be OK, too.

RENTAL AGENCIES

Rental agencies on Chincoteague tend to be locally owned. The background and experience of the owners may be available on the website. We've worked with two over the years, Island Getaways and Chincoteague Resort Vacations, both on Maddox Boulevard. Things have gone well with both. They're helpful and always reachable by phone. If you're renting through Island Getaways, for example, and need something for your trip that won't arrive in time, you can have it shipped to yourself at their office (Nice, right?). Other agencies include Seaside Vacations, Chincoteague Island Vacation Cottages, Eastern Shore Retreats, and Harbour Rentals.

As you consider your accommodation budget, read posted prices carefully. A hefty tax (12.3% in 2021) applies to rentals—a favorite tactic of municipalities with many visitors. Cleaning fees may or may not be included. A credit card processing fee may apply, avoidable by sending a check in advance. On Chincoteague, reservations are generally a necessity. Availability can be tight. Linen rental is additional (and reasonable), as is travel insurance, if you feel the need. Take a few minutes to read what it *doesn't* cover.

- Island Getaways: 7038 Maddox Boulevard, Chincoteague, VA 23336 (757) 336-1236 https://igetaway.net/ Email: igetaway@esva.net
- Chincoteague Resort Vacations: 6426 Maddox Boulevard, Chincoteague, VA 23336 (757) 336-3100 https://www.chincoteagueresort.com/ Email: rentals@chincoteagueresort.com
- Seaside Vacations: 4101 Main Street, Chincoteague, VA 23336 (757) 336-7070 https://www.seasidevacations.rentals/ Email: seasidevacations@email.trackshs.com
- Chincoteague Island Vacation Cottages: 4407 Deep Hole Road, Chincoteague, VA 23336 (757) 336-3720 http://www.chincoteagueislandvacationcottages.com/ Email: vacations@chincoteagueisland.com
- Harbour Rentals: 6455 Maddox Boulevard, Chincoteague, VA 23336 (800) 221-5059 https://www.harbourrentals.net/ Email: harbourrentals@verizon.net

FINDING THE RIGHT RENTAL

You'll probably end up choosing your agency because they list a property you like. Their websites feature detailed descriptions of the home's layout and all-important sleeping arrangements. It's de rigueur to give the property a name, such as "Belle of the Bay" or "Summer Breeze" (occasionally, the names change.) Of course, they all have addresses too. You can search their locations on any online map. Most listings feature dozens of photos—kitchen, bedrooms, common areas, and (drum roll, please) the view. If the home is on the water, you'll find plenty of pictures of its access to the channel or the bay. There's a good chance you can find something that works based on descriptions and photos alone. Agencies welcome an email or call to provide details. Call or email early in the planning stages if you have specific needs, such as access for a person with disabilities or a pet-friendly rental. The rental pros can narrow your search quickly.

They do make a living selling a product. You'll find glowing descriptions of places you're considering. You'll also find enough photos to help you make a good decision. We'd never been surprised at what we found when we arrived. It's a competitive market. Thousands of visitors are looking for accommodations every week. Many return year after year. Word of mouth plays an important role in a "cottage" industry. Odds are you'll be very happy when you open the door to your rental.

· LOCATIONS AND THEIR ADVANTAGES ·

DOWNTOWN

"Downtown" in the small town of Chincoteague describes the cluster of streets between Main Street, along the water (where the swing bridge used to bring folks to town), and Ridge Road, access to the East Side. Maddox Boulevard, farther north, intersects via Chicken City Road. It's a small quadrangle. A downtown rental offers peace and quiet, to be sure. Traffic will be minimal, especially after 9, when most of the Island shutters for the night. A perfect sunset view requires a walk, drive, or bike ride of perhaps three blocks to Robert Reed Park or another good spot, such as Leonard Park across from Chincoteague High School. You're close to the supermarket, the Famer's Market, fun shopping and browsing, the movie theatre, and the church of your choice. It's a good proposition, downtown.

MAIN STREET

Main Street is part of "downtown," a shopping and dining center. Robert Reed Park is a prominent feature. As you travel north or south, you'll find rentals that face the channel, either at the front or back of the home. The payoff? Sunsets. If you're a fan of doing nothing for a half-hour each evening (perhaps with a beverage or a good cigar—forgive my vices, please), while the blazing sky turns to indigo with the setting of the sun, this is a very good area.

We stayed in an excellent rental one year ("Sunny Claire") two doors down from the grand old brick firehouse. The second story featured a glorious sitting porch with a water view. We came to call it "Heaven." If it turns out actual heaven is just like that porch, I think it'd be about right.

WILDCAT MARSH

Traveling north or "up-island" on Main Street, you'll find homes on both sides of the road. On the west side, most feature large windows to take advantage of the channel view. You'll pass the Captain Timothy Hill House, the oldest existing structure on Chincoteague. Soon you'll enter "Wildcat Marsh," the northern tip of the island, where many older homes and cottages have been

Chincoteague's historic downtown retains the character, and many of the buildings, from a century or more ago. The place for shopping and strolling. (Photo by Darcy and Steve Cole, DSC Photography DSCPhotography.net.)

renovated with great care. At the cul-de-sac marked by the 1877 gravesite of Captain Joshua Chandler (leave a coin or a shell), a turn leads to Wildcat Lane and Salt Marsh Lane. Both feature large, newer homes built from the 1980s and onward, accommodating large families or groups with channel access. Some are quite luxurious. They command a premium as rentals.

NORTHEAST SIDE: OYSTER BAY AND LITTLE OYSTER BAY

On the east side of the Island north of downtown, you'll find a variety of mainly modern rental homes available, some with access to the Assateague Channel, or to canals leading to it. Many properties feature boat docks. Here, as on the East Side, you won't get the full effect of the setting sun. This is a particularly quiet part of the Island but still a short drive or bike ride from the places you'll want to go.

PINEY ISLAND

Tucked into the eastern shore of Chincoteague Island, off Maddox Boulevard near the Beach Road bridge to Assateague, is the Piney Island section. It's not an "island" in the standard sense. Piney Island is its own little area, quiet but very close to Maddox Boulevard (the Main Drag)

The oversized "love chairs" with one of the commercial fishing vessels that still ply surrounding waters. (Photo by Darcy and Steve Cole, DSC Photography DSCPhotography.net.)

The centerpiece of Robert Reed Park, waterside, downtown. (Photo by Darcy and Steve Cole, DSC Photography DSCPhotography.net.)

Misty, memorialized in bronze on historic Main Street, helped make Chincoteague a destination for generations of visitors. (Photo by Darcy and Steve Cole, DSC Photography DSCPhotography.net.)

and the beach. You'll find many rentals waterside or with access to the water, some with piers for crabbing and boating. As with other areas facing east, the full effect of the sunset isn't felt on Piney Island, but the sunrise will greet you.

EAST SIDE

The East Side of Chincoteague faces undeveloped Assateague, home of the ponies, The Chincoteague Wildlife Refuge, and the famous lighthouse often captured in local art. The Assateague Channel, a wide stretch of water divided by nature into winding and interlocking threads whose levels rise and fall with the tide, provides waterfront access. Sunsets here aren't in their full glory as they are on Chincoteague Bay to the west, but the East Side is a favorite place to kayak, canoe, and crab. You'll find multi-unit "condo-style" residences available as rentals. They're usually listed by unit. The East Side is quiet and very close to downtown. It's home to Veteran's Memorial Park on Eastside Road, featuring really good play equipment, tennis and basketball, a skate park, a boat ramp, and a fishing pier where no license is required.

· CAMPING ·

We haven't camped on Chincoteague, or camped at all except during school, when we backpacked in New Hampshire and Maine, and more recently during my son's days as a Scout. Campers, we admire your courage and flexibility in dealing with all the issues that can arise when you're not indoors: heat and humidity, bugs, weather, and the logistics of managing equipment. Pop-up and tent aficionados like to point out that a modern RV approximates "indoors." Sure—approximately. We still admire you, however you camp. Camping can be hit-or-miss, and yet, you roll with it!

On Chincoteague, three popular campgrounds attract tents, pop-ups, and RVs of all kinds. None are "walking distance" to the most popular Island spots. The KOA facility just off the Maddox Boulevard traffic circle is close to some eating places, a Family Dollar, and an Ace Home Center, but Maddox is not very walkable. It's a busy two-lane road, and businesses are somewhat spread out. One of the best things about Chincoteague is its bike-friendliness; if you're willing to put in a few miles on a bike, everything is accessible from all three campgrounds. All are also a stop on the old-style Chincoteague Trolley, the "Pony Express," that travels many of the most popular places on the Island for just half a buck per person.

Tom's Cove is a very large and old campground with literally hundreds of campsites. Many adult campers first visited there as kids. The rambling site on Beebe Road near the south end of Chincoteague Island is just a mile or so from Curtis Merritt Harbor, where boats and many charters dock. It's also very close to Veteran's Memorial Park, a nice recreation spot for kids. Tom's Cove features three fishing piers and a boat ramp of its own, along with a pool, a playground, a laundromat, and a store.

Tom's Cove does business the old-fashioned way—probably much like it has from the start. You download a reservation form online at tomscovepark.com, but from there, the process goes full analog in a hurry: you complete the form with a pen and mail it to them with a deposit check (you can also just write them a letter with all the details). You can't reserve online or even by phone. It's mail-in only. They'll mail you back a confirmation. The deposit is refundable up to two weeks before arrival.

Tom's Cove doesn't take credit cards to pay the site fee, either. Cash, personal check, or traveler's check. I haven't seen a traveler's check in a while, but they're still available and still have the illustration of that noble-looking Roman soldier, or whatever he is.

The Chincoteague Island KOA (formerly Maddox Family Campground) is just off the Maddox Boulevard traffic circle, adjacent to the new (2019) Maui Jack's Waterpark. It's a big campground, with a location right in the thick of things on Maddox, and very close to the entrance to Chincoteague National Wildlife Refuge. If you plan to travel by bike to do your activities, this is a convenient spot. On the flip side, it's the least 'secluded' on the Island. Campers have a lot of choices in addition to campsites. You can reserve rental RV's, cabins, small "Island Bungalows," and large glamping-style safari tents. As part of the huge KOA network, the campground benefits from a sophisticated online reservation system that allows you to specify exactly what sort of site you need and when. Reservations can be made immediately.

Though Maui Jack's Waterpark is adjacent to the KOA (it was built on a portion of the site of the former Maddox Family Campground), admission isn't included in your stay. You do get a discount.

The Pine Grove Campground and Waterfowl Park off Deep Hole Road towards the north end of Chincoteague (right next to the excellent Gary Howard Seafood market) is the most eccentric of the three, and at 37 acres, the smallest. It's in a quiet area. Located in a grove of yellow pines (as you might expect), the property features six ponds, often home to Island birdlife. The campground also has a peacock—not a native bird, of course, but a resident, nonetheless. There's a dock for crabbing and a public boat launch nearly. Campground features include a pool, a laundromat, and a camp store. Motel-style units and cottage apartments are available in addition to traditional tent and RV sites. You can reserve by phone using a credit card.

One characteristic of Island topography is worth pointing out: Chincoteague is pretty much all at sea level and doesn't drain well (the town lacks a central sewer system, but relies on individual septic systems). You may go to sleep in a dry, sandy campsite and wake up to large puddles after heavy overnight rainfall.

* Tom's Cove Campground: PO Box 122, 8128 Beebe Road, Chincoteague, VA 23336 (757) 336-6498 https://tomscovepark.com/
  Email: tomscovepark@verizon.net

* Chincoteague Island KOA: 6742 Maddox Boulevard, Chincoteague, VA 23336 (757) 336-3111 Reservations: (800) 562-7730
  https://koa.com/campgrounds/chincoteague/
  Email: chincoteague@koa.com

* Pine Grove Campground: 5283 Deep Hole Road, Chincoteague, VA 23336 (757) 336-5200 https://www.chincoteaguepinegrove.com/
  Email: PineGroveVA@gmail.com

▪ STAYING OFF THE ISLAND ▪

I wouldn't rule out staying off the Island if you see accommodations more as a place to lay your head than part of the trip's appeal. Traffic is manageable except at peak times on big beach days when beachgoers exit en masse. It's a two-lane road, and everyone is headed to the same place—the causeway. Several traffic lights and many local businesses (some with popular drive-throughs) fall in between. You won't get caught in a New-Jersey-style traffic jam, but it may take a while. If you can time your beach exit a little before or after everyone else, that's in your favor. The attractions of the Island (including the beach) are so easily accessed that the relatively short additional travel time doesn't put a big wrinkle in your day.

The nearest cluster of chain hotels is in Salisbury, Maryland, 48 miles and over an hour away. There's a Holiday Inn Express, an EconoLodge, and an America's Best Value Inn in Pocomoke, Maryland, a half-hour trip. Two bed-and-breakfasts, Chanceford Hall in Snow Hill and The Inn at Onancock, are close by.

Prices fall as you leave Chincoteague. The trade-off is the loss of a quiet place to regroup during the day (especially when weather doesn't cooperate) and the chance to wind down in the evening with sunsets, ice cream, and a stroll down by the water close to your bed.

ISLAND VOICES

RUTHANN MASON, THE WATERSIDE INN

Like so many, the story of Ruthann Mason's journey to Chincoteague is a love story. "I came here with a friend on vacation," she related. We stayed at that lovely Victorian home across Main Street. I went on a double date at the carnival grounds. We've been together ever since. We were married in 1995."

The Waterside Inn was built in 1987. Ruthann began working at the front desk in 1992. "We have 45 rooms and four condos," she pointed out. "It's a family business. We want people to enjoy themselves on a beach vacation. I'm really grateful to be on vacation when I go away. I believe in 'Give 'em the Pickle,'"

Ruthann Mason of the Waterside Inn, Chincoteague.

said Ruthann, quoting the best-selling inspiration book on business by Bob Ferrell. "We started here before any of the national chains arrived. We want to be different and special in our own way because we're not part of a big corporation. Guests notice. They come back again and again. People who first stayed here as children are bringing their own children."

"Chincoteague is a wonderful place to raise kids," Ruthann told me. "We have two sons. I was President of the PTA when they were in grade school, then headed up the after-prom committee." She was also co-founder of the town's February Death by Chocolate event in 2006. "It's a lot of fun. This is a perfect place to celebrate Thanksgiving with family, too. And we have a really good time at Christmas."

Long-time Chincoteague residents have fond memories of vanished landmarks. "The Crab House, the Shucking House Café, Captain Fish's, The Chincoteague

Inn. There have been a lot of changes. Change can be good. We have to be sure it's sustainable and know how much is too much. The family businesses here have built a strong foundation. Our long-term employees are very important to us. Some of our housekeepers travel 45 minutes to get here."

The sudden changes brought on by the COVID pandemic were especially tough for hotels. "We had to re-evaluate everything about how we run our business," said Ruthann. "Everyone misses our big breakfast buffet right in the lobby. We hope we can bring that back soon. This year, we've been short-staffed all season, like nearly every business. We're all working harder than ever. It does make it more difficult to give everyone your best. We really appreciate it when people are patient."

A hotelkeeper may be the perfect person to offer travelers advice. "We absolutely love to fulfill special requests," Ruthann told me. "There are only a few of us here. You can talk to us about whatever you need: your schedule, the room you prefer, whatever you like! Our family is helping your family. The earlier you plan your trip and make reservations, the more we can do for you and happier you'll be on Chincoteague."

WHERE TO EAT

· LOCAL RESTAURANTS: BRICK AND MORTAR ·

Full disclosure: we haven't eaten a lot of meals at traditional restaurants on Chincoteague. We've had good experiences at several. We strongly support good local restaurants (like all local businesses), especially family-owned ones. Their numbers are dwindling. By all means, go out to eat at those that appeal to you.

Sit-down restaurants are not my strong suit. Our fairly large family rents a home when visiting the Island. We're able to bring takeout food home and cook. We often do both. Lines at take-out places can be long—but only one person needs to make the food run. Hungry kids, not known for patience, do better at home than waiting for food to arrive at their table. And, while it's work to prepare a meal, it's a labor of love with ingredients this good. I first tried my hand at traditional Eastern Shore crab cakes with crabmeat fresh from Gary Howard Seafood on Deep Hole Road. I like to think I get a little better at it every year—but just as a bad day fishin' is better than a good day workin', even an imperfect crab cake is a better meal than most.

Chincoteague merits its own "foodies" group on Facebook ("Chincoteague Island Foodies," 10,000 members as of February 2022). Many new eateries aren't brick-and-mortar, but several traditional restaurants boast longevity and a loyal following. If sit-down dining is your preference, you'll do well to look into Bill's Prime, Don's Seafood Restaurant, AJ's on the Creek, Ray's Shanty (15 minutes off-island in Wattsville), and Steamers Sports Bar. They're often mentioned as favorites. Each has its personality, some very different from others.

Steamers is a bustling, fun place, with an emphasis on filling your plate with fresh local seafood: "great food in ample portions." You may find the game you were hoping to catch on one of the many big screens.

Bill's Prime (on Main Street next to the old Chincoteague firehouse) is easily the most ambitious on the island. It's a lovely, small, traditional dining spot—probably the most-recommended destination for special occasions. AJ's also falls into that category—a calm, breezy, informal restaurant in the perfect spot on Eel Creek by the Assateague Bridge. (AJ's was founded in 1985 by AJ Stillson, a jazz pianist. Their email should be a tip-off.) They're now doing all-day brunch Fridays and Saturdays.

Don's has been a veritable fixture downtown since the early 1970s and a dependable destination for signature seafood. Their oysters come from Tom's Cove Aquafarms—a big plus. Tommy Clark, the owner of Don's, started Tom's Cove in 1999.

Ray's Shanty is the sort of big, old-fashioned wood-paneled local place you don't often see anymore. Captain Ray and his wife Laura have run it since 1986. One door leads to the dining room, another to the seafood market. Passing it quickly on Route 175 (Chincoteague Road), you might not realize the unadorned green two-story building is even a restaurant.

All are often reviewed on well-known sites such as Yelp and TripAdvisor. You'll find hundreds, even thousands, of opinions. A little research should quickly reveal which suits your taste that day.

You can enjoy a white-tablecloth experience on the island. Depending on the sort of dining you're used to, you may need to be a bit flexible. Anyone who's worked in food service will tell you no restaurant is at its best on a very busy night. In Chincoteague Memorial Day through Labor Day, many nights are. Dining rooms are often crowded. While this doesn't create the logjams routine in bigger resort towns, it may not be the ideal recipe for an idyllic evening out.

It isn't uncommon for restaurants to be short-staffed. A "reservation" may not mean what it does at a place with a more predictable traffic flow. In short, you might need to bring some patience with your appetite. When you read a negative review of a Chincoteague restaurant, difficulty with service is often the reason. That's usually caused by the crush of business during the season. If you're used to Martha's Vineyard, the Cape, Long Island, or any number of resort areas, you're familiar.

A fine-dining atmosphere isn't the main attraction on Chincoteague. It's an informal place by nature (many visitors don't pack dressy clothes or shoes). Even a very nice restaurant on a good night may not offer the ambiance to which you're accustomed.

Consider menu choices given the location. Resist the urge to get too fancy. The town made its living from the ocean for a couple of centuries. You can't find this kind of seafood just anywhere. You have the chance to enjoy it the way it's been enjoyed in the region pretty much forever. Let the fish and shellfish play the starring roles.

The island is home to many more "every day" restaurants that are anything but. The Village, Etta's Channel Side, Beach Road Round-up, ChincoTiki, Ropewalk, Teaguer's, Maria's, Mr. Baldy's (known for its breakfast—you have tried scrapple, haven't you?), and Saigon Village (Among the few Asian-food choices—well-established on the Island and quite good. It can be tough to reach them. Maybe just stop by) are local favorites. Many are open in the off-season when others aren't. Most feature a more general menu with a broader focus, still built around excellent seafood. While the surroundings may be simpler, you'll find exceptional food. Those opening earlier in the day are great choices for breakfast and lunch. In general, these restaurants don't impress from the outside. That's not where they spend their money. Try them. You'll be glad you did.

On Chincoteague, every restaurant gets plenty of out-of-town visitors and abundant reviews on popular websites like TripAdvisor and Yelp. That's a big assist when faced with many choices. You'll find a lot of enthusiasm for their personal attention to the customer. These are typically home-town, family-owned businesses, often under the same ownership for decades. Some are a little off the beaten path (the "beaten path" being Maddox Boulevard and Main Street). On Chincoteague, nothing is far from anything else. During peak days and times, lines tend to be way shorter. Don't hesitate to give traditional local restaurants a try for any meal.

You'll even find a McDonalds and a Subway on Maddox Boulevard—but you can eat at one anytime. Famous Pizza and Sub Shop, also on Maddox, will gladly make you a local sub, as will J & B Subs, a very popular 50-year-old year-round local business a short drive down South Main that makes its own sides and lets you choose your own dill pickle. If you're from Philly and a cheesesteak is calling your name, that's their #1 seller. It's not a glamorous place, but the subs are great. It's neat as a pin, and they're happy to see you.

♦ Bill's Prime: 4040 Main Street, Chincoteague, VA 23336 (757) 336-5831
https://www.billsseafoodrestaurant.com/ Email: Info@BillsPrime.com

- Don's Seafood Restaurant: 4113 Main Street, Chincoteague, VA 23336 (757) 336-5715 https://www.donsseafoodrestaurant.com/ Email: contact@DonSeafoodRestaurant.com

- AJ's on the Creek: 6585 Maddox Boulevard, Chincoteague, VA 23336 (757) 894-7209 https://www.ajsotc.com/ Email: Blueseaandbird@gmail.com

- Steamers Sports Bar: 6251 Maddox Boulevard, Chincoteague, VA 23336 (757) 336-5300 https://steamerschincoteague.com/ Email: info@SteamersChincoteague.com

- Ray's Shanty: PO Box 13, 32157 Chincoteague Road, Wattsville, VA 23483 (757) 824-3429 http://www.raysshanty.com/ Email: Ray-Laura@RaysShanty.com

- The Village Restaurant: 6576 Maddox Boulevard, Chincoteague VA 23336 (757) 336-5120 https://www.chincoteague.com/thevillage/

- Etta's Channel Side: 7452 East Side Drive, Chincoteague VA 23336 (757) 336-5644 https://www.ettaschannelside.com/ Email: jangow@verizon.net

- Beach Road Roundup: 6341 Maddox Boulevard, Chincoteague VA 23336 (757) 336-0617 https://beachroadroundup.business.site/ Email: beachroadroundup@gmail.com

- ChincoTiki: 4121 Main Street, Chincoteague VA 23336 (757) 336-1111 http://chincotiki.weebly.com/ Email: jordsee@gmail.com

- Ropewalk: 6262 Marlin Street, Chincoteague, VA 23336 (757) 336-1111 https://chincoteague.ropewalk.com/ Email: jason@ropewalk.com

- Teaguer's: 5030 Chicken City Road, Chincoteague, VA 23336 (757) 336-7237 https://teaguerspub.wixsite.com/my-site Email: Teaguerspub@hotmail.com

- Maria's: 6506 Maddox Boulevard, Chincoteague, VA 23336 (757) 336-5040 https://www.facebook.com/MariasChincoteague/

- Mr. Baldy's: 3441 Ridge Road, Chincoteague, VA 23336 (757) 336-1198 https://www.chincoteaguechamber.com/directory/mr-baldys-family-restaurant/ Email: mah73@hotmail.com

- Saigon Village: 4069 Main Street, Chincoteague, VA 23336 (757) 336-0584 https://www.saigonvillagechincoteague.com/

TOM CLARK, DON'S SEAFOOD RESTAURANT AND TOM'S COVE AQUA FARMS

Not many Chincoteague Island businesses pre-date Don's Seafood Restaurant on Main Street downtown: it's due to celebrate its 50th anniversary in just a couple of years, in a difficult industry known for rapid change, owner Tom Clark and his daughter Anne have stuck with the same approach over time—the same one Tom's father took in 1973. "You make it work one day at a time," Tom told me. "We feature the best seafood we can, as local as we can get it, made the old Chincoteague way. Find some of the old cookbooks the local churches used to sell as fundraisers. People on the Island have always known how to make seafood interest-

Tommy Clark, Don's Seafood Restaurant and Tom's Cove Aqua Farms.

ing." The flounder is local. Tom farms the clams and oysters at his other enterprise, Tom's Cove Aqua Farms. The scallops are from New Bedford, the shrimp from Texas and the Carolinas. Tom sources that way for a good reason. "They cost more than the imported stuff, but they're better, and I want every American to keep their jobs, especially watermen."

Chincoteague used to support many, many watermen, but the picture changed in the 1960s and 1970s, as the oyster industry declined and permitting regulations tightened. Now, it's harder to make a living on the water. Only a handful of Island-ers do so. As tourism supplanted seafood as Chincoteague's main revenue source, Don's Seafood Restaurant became a favorite destination for many families. "It's just a habit with me, even though I'm officially a Grumpy Old Man now," Tom told me. "Good food and reasonable prices. We've had customers bring their kids, and then those kids bring grandkids."

Tom is especially grateful for the staff of over 50 that makes the restaurant run. "We have a core of 30 veterans, some as long as 25 years," he said. "The dedication and work ethic of those long-term staffers makes the business enjoyable." Tom agrees with many folks in his industry that the whole country would benefit if everyone had to wait tables at least once in their lives.

Increasingly, younger Chincoteaguers are leaving the Island for career oppor-tunities and because local real estate is booming, making it tough to find a first home. "Sometimes I wish my daughter Anne had gone over to NASA—steady income, benefits, 9 to 5. But she loves doing this," Tom told me. Anne has already put her stamp on the restaurant, opening its new outdoor dining pavilion, "Don's Daughter." She's the third generation at Don's.

The clams and oysters on the menu at Don's Seafood Restaurant are pretty special. "I've worked with clams and oysters all my life," Tom recalled. "I farmed them as a hobby. One year they did great, the next not so well. The restaurant used to slow down early in September. In 1999 I took a course at the Harbor Branch Oceanographic Institute in Florida. I set up oysters in my backyard. Had to make my own seawater. Pretty soon, I learned how not to kill them so fast. We started Tom's Cove Aqua Farms in 2000. It took off pretty fast." Tom's Cove is up to 12 employees now. It's part of a clam co-operative with 15 other aquafarmers. 99% of their products are shipped off the Island, some as far away as the Grand Central Oyster Bar in Manhattan. He's continuing in a trade that sustained the Island for much of its history. "Plant a tomato," Tom pointed out, "It's ready in three months. An oyster, three years. That discourages a lot of people." Tom encourages oyster fans to bring the shells back for re-planting in the sea. Over the years, using them for their mineral content, or paving roads and driveways, had a devastating effect on the oyster population. Today, shells are being collected and re-planted. "My own driveway," said Tom, "Is paved with stones."

Danny Berry captains a thirty-foot dredge boat at Tom's Cove. "I work hard," he said, "But I love it." Every young waterman dreams of becoming a first mate, then captain of his own boat. Danny worked his way up. Then the boats began leaving for New Jersey. He followed them, captaining there as well. "I made good money," he told me, "But I got tired of it there. Too many people, and they're different. They don't have the regard for one another people do here."

Danny understands why people like to visit Chincoteague. "It's perfect here. God's country. Get out on a boat and see it up close." Tom agreed. "Slow down and relax," he advised. "It's the attitude of the people that makes the Island what it is. Take your time. Where are you going anyway? You'll soon come to appreciate what we have here and what it took to get it there."

▪ SEA STAR ▪

Sea Star, it seems like we've known you forever. How many Tabbouleh Wraps ago did we meet? We remember the occasion well—though not the date. It might have been 2005. You were just a little place in those days, squashed into that former ice-cream stand, or whatever it was, off Main Street. The oyster-shell parking lot held maybe three cars. With the old screens and jalousie windows in the way, it was tough even to see faces, but still, we knew we'd found something special. We knew as soon as we tasted your Tabbouleh Wraps: ultra-fresh, minty tabbouleh, garlicky hummus, ripe red tomatoes, and crisp romaine. The perfect vegetarian—vegan, even—healthy beach lunch. Your peach and raspberry iced tea refreshed us, your black forest ham and brie on a croissant nourished us, and your smoked turkey with Havarti on sourdough piqued our interest. Alas, so many waited at your tiny window you barely acknowledged us. You moved on to the next in line, leaving us hungry for more.

Then, one day, we found your little cottage empty. We despaired until we came upon your sign in a newer, bigger place, right off Maddox, near Chicken City Road. We called on you again, this time in a bigger lot, with a longer line, but with a shaded porch and a big pond out back, where a Snowy Egret always seemed to be fishing. Our love was as strong as ever.

We can seldom eat the sandwiches at one sitting. The bread is phenomenal, the construction all your own. We've taken home "Tab Wraps" (our nickname) and deconstructed them so that we could make them ourselves. We can't. Only you can, somehow. We can't give you up, Sea Star.

♦ Sea Star: 6439 Maddox Boulevard, Chincoteague, VA 23336
(757) 336-5442 http://seastarcafeci.com/

▪ FOOD TRUCKS: MANY AND VARIED ▪

Chincoteague food trucks are a new development—and a very good one. Why food trucks? Building a brick-and-mortar restaurant on Chincoteague is a difficult undertaking. For one thing, the island is just a little above sea level and has no central sewage system. (The typical residence has a septic tank with a concrete cover, known as a "Chincoteague Patio.") An ideal solution is a food truck that can dispose of its limited wastewater elsewhere.

Some of the food trucks on the Island look like the ones you're used to. Some don't. Ingenious restaurateurs have incorporated awnings, fences, outdoor seating, and fun décor that distracts attention from the mobile nature of the food preparation vehicle itself. Woody's, a very good barbeque place just west of the traffic circle, is a fine example. Others, such as the new-for 2021 Blackfin, specializing in poke bowls, make no effort to hide their food-truck status: Blackfin operates out of a converted aqua-blue New York City school bus. Each season brings new ones.

WOODY'S SERIOUS FOOD

Woody's was The First of the Food Trucks, according to Larry Parsons, who started it and still runs it. From Maddox Boulevard, Woody's doesn't look like a food truck per se. It's better described as a "complex." The big sandy lot just off the traffic circle contains a wooden storage shack with a big Day-Glo peace sign, a VW bus, a vintage motorboat, a cluster of hammocks, and some (I believe) unwinnable games to pass the time while your order is prepared. A corrugated tin roof festooned with surfboards covers the ordering and pickup area. The whole vibe is a beach joint in the Caribbean, Reggae music and all. Only when you look closely do you see how it all fits together. Everything, including the massive smokers and the pile of hardwood out back, is clustered around a single mobile trailer kitchen—in other words, a food truck.

For Southerners, barbeque can be a touchy topic. It's a lot like pizza to New Yorkers—everyone has preferences and favorites. One man's meat is another man's . . . inferior meat. What makes great barbecue? Deeply held convictions vary. You pay your money, and you take your choice of sauce and sides. All that said, we really like Woody's and always have. It's very good barbecue. The price is right. And the crew cares about getting you your food as fast as they can—not very fast, at peak times. They can't help that. It's an extremely popular place.

The menu is solid: pulled pork, ribs, half-chickens, and chicken chunks, with several sauces. Only brisket is missing. The usual suspects are among the delicious sides: fries, baked beans, coleslaw, and a famous outlier—corn nuggets, addictive fried nibblers with excellent yum-yum sauce (I've tried to make them at home. Got close, but no Woody's). Order some or regret it. Big Family Packs can provide dinner and leftovers for tomorrow's lunch if your group is large.

With us, Woody's, like Captain Zack's, is kind of a staple—even a ritual. *When is Woody's night?* It's bound to be one of them. Probably more than one. Not bad for a place on wheels, right?

✦ Woody's Serious Food: 6700 Maddox Boulevard, Chincoteague, VA 23336 (410) 430-4429 https://www.woodysseriousfood.com/ Email: gotdrums@msn.com

ISLAND VOICES

LARRY PARSONS, WOODY'S SERIOUS FOOD

As the opening day of Woody's Serious Food approached, things didn't look so good for "Woody" (Larry Parsons of Chincoteague, formerly of Pocomoke, Maryland). He stopped into Don's Restaurant and overheard some long-time residents conversing over breakfast. "I hear some idiot is opening a barbeque place on Maddox," one said (Who would do that in a seafood town?). He drove to the sandy lot he leased from a local owner many months before, when it was covered with phragmites, brush, and weeds. As he unhooked the chain at the entrance to the lot, he noticed that the parking area at the Ace Home Center across the traffic circle was full. Odd. Maybe they were having a big sale? Nope—all the cars followed him into the lot at Woody's. They wanted barbeque. The year was 2007.

Larry Parsons (left) of Woody's Serious Food, with a happy customer.

"It was a tipping point," Larry said, "right from the very start. It's never one thing that makes it work; it's a combination of things." Woody's, his brainchild, was the First Food Truck on Chincoteague Island, beginning a big trend. Today, t's arguably the most visible place to eat on an island that boasts so many good ones, but Larry had to make up the rules as he went along. As they say, he took the leap, hoping to sprout wings on the way down. And he did.

He'd heard about all-star chefs, tired of watching restaurant owners pocketing big profits, opening food trucks in L.A., with lines around the block. He knew something like that could work on Chincoteague. Though he had a vision right from the start of what "Woody's" would bring to the Island. It was a tough sell to the City Fathers. A food truck? Nobody had ever done it. They weren't sure about an outdoor smoker. What about the smell? "In the barbeque business," Larry countered, "We don't call it smell. We call it aroma." And the reggae music, a fond memory from Larry's sojourn in Negril, Jamaica, in the 1970s? Would it disturb beachgoers on their way to Assateague? He'd have to put in his own septic system, too. The obstacles were many.

It wasn't the first rodeo for the son of a hotelier from Pocomoke. His family had operated a 90-room Best Western with a white-tablecloth dining room that featured a pianist on weekends. When the hotel was sold, he opened a fitness center. He was also a musician from his teenage years—a drummer who played in local ensembles, including a ten-piece James Brown tribute band. He loved the pace of Washington, DC, and New York City. He still does, and visits when time permits. "After about ten days," Larry said, "Get me back here, where I don't even remember where the keys to the locks are." He wanted a business on Chincoteague.

He remembered Cherry's Restaurant, if you could call it that, from Negril: half an oil drum for making jerk chicken, a big tub of Red Stripe beer on ice, and a picnic table so rickety he didn't even want to try sitting on it. There was nothing to it, really, but the food was outstanding, and it was fun. He didn't want to serve beer—Woody's would be a family place (old-fashioned Boylan's soda fit right in), but all the key ingredients would be there: great food, a location close to the beach, music, atmosphere, fun, and, above all, the personal attention of the owner. It all mattered. "People need only two things when they travel—a place to stay and somewhere to eat," Larry told me. "Anyone can feed people—but can you make it fun?"

He convinced the town and got his permit. Now, he had to make it work. He and his wife moved to a tiny house on the Island. He made calls, first to a friend who'd graduated from culinary school and was interning in a 5-star property on Sea Island, Georgia. The friend was skeptical, but in the end, he was in and gave his two weeks' notice. It turned out the head chef wasn't happy with the restaurant's barbecue sauce. He directed his intern to spend his two remaining weeks creating a better one. If it proved worthy, he could take it with him. He did. That's been Woody's signature sauce for 15 years.

Over time, Larry perfected his barbecue method. His pork is on the smoker for 20 hours—3 in the smoke, the rest wrapped in foil. "Three hours gives it all the smoke it can take," he said. He stays in a motor home on the Woody's complex (technically part of the adjacent KOA) and gets out of bed every four hours to feed the smoker. When it's done, the meat falls off the bone. Order ribs. Your first one will tell the tale.

He's had the same wood supplier from the start, a Pocomoke mill owner who brings him red oak, hickory, and cherrywood. He uses the "best ingredients I can get my hands on." A supplier once told him he could get him something cheaper. "Unless it's your best stuff cheaper," he answered, "Don't even use that word."

Larry isn't interested in competing or winning awards for his work. "If I want a trophy with a pig on it," he said, "I'll go buy myself one." His best review came from a customer who stayed on Chincoteague for a week and ate nine times at Woody's.

Woody's, an outdoor dining and takeout venue exclusively, has come through the pandemic in good shape so far. Parsons walked the lot with a tape measure and rearranged everything 6' apart. He changes things up from time to time in the Woody's complex in other ways, too. He's added a circle of hammocks to his trademark games (he insisted the ring-on-the-hook game is winnable) to help waiting customers pass the time more pleasantly. On occasion, when lines are very long, he brings out a tub of watermelon slices on ice.

The biggest challenge at Woody's recently has been people. The customers come back again and again, but staff are in short supply. Parsons will hire any Chincoteaguers who want to work. Before the pandemic, young people from all over the world sought out summer employment on the Island. He would take them on a day-long outing to New York or DC at season's end. All that is on hold now. During the 2021 season, Woody's often endured unprecedented rolling shutdowns because only Larry and a tiny cohort of employees reported.

He's even got an online delivery system, similar to Door Dash, ready to launch as soon as drivers want to sign on. He's not going to put the plan in motion until he can do it consistently well. "I respect McDonald's," he said. "In New York or

Singapore, when you order a Big Mac, you know it will be consistent." That's a hallmark of Woody's. From year to year, visitors to the Island know they'll deliver.

So how did Larry Parsons become 'Woody?' The nickname isn't his, rightly. The restaurant was named to honor and remember a relative who died in a tragic accident years ago. From the outset, diners would ask who "Woody" was. Larry hesitated to tell the sad story of the young man. One spring, the first customer asked, "Are you Woody?"

"It was only hard the first time," he admitted. "I said, 'That's me.'"

He's been Woody ever since, all over the Island, and in innumerable selfies. A customer even spotted him at an airport in Mexico.

"The more I give, the more I get," Larry told me. The well-known restaurateur still performs on the drums. Among his most treasured gigs were the Sunday services at the Church of God across the traffic circle from Woody's. He worked in youth ministry, too. Everything he's done involves serving the public. "I'm not money-driven," he told me. "Some years I do better, some worse. I'm driven to make what I've got the best it can possibly be. If you're driven by money first, it won't work."

"Woody," owner of the first food truck on Chincoteague, isn't too concerned when people claim the Island will 'turn into Ocean City.' He had only one question: "How?"

"BETTER."

Name all the restaurants that rose to fame on the strength of their Brussels sprouts. Take all the time you need. See? Yet, when Chef Justin Kerchner and his family opened their food truck, simply named "Better," on Maddox Boulevard in 2019, that's what had folks raving: deep-fried Brussels sprouts drizzled with balsamic vinegar. *Couldn't even get them home before eating them!*" *Had to buy two the next time!*" They also loved the Potato Rocket (a continuous spiral of potato, on a stick), the crab cakes, the chowder, the Caprese salad, the burger, and the schnitzel. This is lovingly chef-crafted food made with good, fresh ingredients. It actually IS Better. It's not "island food" or even "vacation food," per se. If I could offer the Chef advice, it might be to lean the menu a little more in that direction. But if you're picking up what Justin is putting down, you can't find it done better than he does. Also, for what it's worth, Justin's laser-cut steel chef's knife logo is the second coolest on the Island. Bravo, Chef!

♦ Better.: 6507 Maddox Boulevard, Chincoteague, VA 23336
(757) 894-8153 https://betterfoodtruck.net/
Email: foodtruck.better@gmail.com

PICO TAQUERIA

Pico Taqueria used to be a food truck, small and very busy. Now they have a brick-and-mortar-home, a bar, and outdoor and indoor seating, so they're larger, and very busy. You can't call ahead or order online. You stand in line and place your order personally. You get a buzzer, like at Olive Garden. At busy times (surprisingly often, even on weekdays), 20 to 40 minutes is typical. The taco and taco bowl aficionados in our family are all thumbs up for Pico, "the real deal." It's fresh and flavorful. The guac and chips are handmade. Don't leave without the Eastern Shore Street Corn: corn on the cob with butter, Old Bay seasoning, melted shredded cheese, and parsley. The tacos don't demand cheese if cheese isn't your thing.

The staff is more than helpful. They'll cook to order for those with food sensitivities. They seem happy to see you, no matter how busy, which is saying something. Menu prices are odd numbers (like $5.21), so tax brings it up to a round number, and they don't have to make change. Maybe this helps keep them so mellow.

Pico—and tacos in general—seem popular with people exiting the beach. That's a good time to avoid if you're flexible. The food travels well if you won't be home for a while. Like many places on the Island, Pico maintains a schedule with rolling closures, perhaps more so than other places. The Pico rooster gets our vote for the coolest logo on the Island, for what it's worth.

+ Pico Taqueria: 6560 Maddox Boulevard, Chincoteague, VA 23336
  (757) 894-8153 https://picotaqueria.com/
  Email: Info@Picotaqueria.com

LILY'S LITTLE MEXICO

Here's my dilemma: the taco people in our group are Pico people, so we have no experience with Lily's. The people who do just love the place and say so online with great enthusiasm—the food, the staff, the whole setup. As Pico used to be, Lily's is a food truck on Maddox near the traffic circle, close to Woody's, a favorite stop to or from the beach. Reviews are consistently excellent, often mentioning the authenticity of the food. Those who've dined in Mexico are reminded of that experience. The menu includes tacos, sopes, quesadillas, burritos, fajitas, and tostadas.

+ Lily's Little Mexico: 6700 Maddox Boulevard, Chincoteague, VA 23336
  (757) 894-0754 https://www.facebook.com/lilyslittlemx/
  Email: lilyslittlemexico@gmail.com

TACO LOCO

A new player on the food-truck scene for 2021, Taco Loco stresses authenticity, variety, and value. The menu isn't complex but offers plenty of choices. Considering it's known for seafood and traditional Southern cooking, Chincoteague offers an embarrassment of riches for Mexican food fans. I suggest taking home selections from all the places and doing a blind tasting. Award points and everything. Tally it all up. It'll be fun. At these prices, why the heck not?

◆ Taco Loco: 6527 Maddox Boulevard, Chincoteague, VA 23336
  (757) 894-8440 https://www.facebook.com/Taco-Loco-104441424666497/

COSA PIZZA

Americans feel more strongly about pizza than probably any other food. If you're from pizza territory, arguably New York/New Jersey/Philly and environs, you've got favorite styles and pizza joints. Our family hails from a pizza-centric area, where several distinctive varieties attract fans. The South is not the place to get picky about pizza, though many beach towns have a place or two that put out a good product.

On Chincoteague, Famous Pizza and Subs, along with Ledo Pizza (a chain active in seven states), have long held down the pizza scene. Many local folks swear by Famous. Ledo is good commercial pizza, a welcome choice for families. It saved our evening a few times when we wanted something simple. Cosa is something altogether new to the Island, most likely the region: a food truck with a 700-degree mobile wood-fired pizza oven. This is serious thin-crust Neapolitan pizza, with the char and big dough blisters you've come to expect from a real wood-fired oven. The ingredients are the real deal, too: tomatoes, mozzarella, sausage, and pro-sciutto. If you love this sort of pizza, chances are you're a little demanding. Give Cosa a try. It's a good thing to find here, right? Do yourself a favor, though: contact them and pre-order. You can't usually just walk up and get a pizza. That's how things are going for Cosa. A good sign.

◆ Cosa Pizza: 6175 Maddox Boulevard, Chincoteague, VA 23336
  (757) 336-7193 https://www.cosapizza.com/
  Email: cosapizzava@gmail.com

SANDY PONY DONUTS

Not long after Sugarbaker's bit the dust, Sandy Pony Donuts arrived. They're a food truck—one of the first to join a movement that's driving the Chincoteague food scene. They began in 2015 in the Atlantic Shoals Surf Shop parking lot on the traffic circle. Their most recent location is also on Maddox, near the well-known H & H Pharmacy. Since their first truck on Chincoteague, they've expanded to four locations in Maryland and Virginia and now offer acai bowls and smoothies. They make cake doughnuts (not the soft raised doughnuts many prefer), on the smaller side, and chewy, as cake doughnuts are. These are "artisanal" doughnuts. I think they're very good—but I like cake doughnuts. They feature exotic icings and toppings: pretzel, blueberry, banana, mint, and fruity pebbles combos. And yes, they have gluten-free donuts. They're excellent. More power to them! The folks who started Sandy Pony know what they're doing.

✦ Sandy Pony Donuts: 6276 Maddox Boulevard, Chincoteague, VA 23336 (757) 336-7246 http://sandyponydonut.com/ Email: info@sandyponydonut.com

BACKYARD FIREPIT

So, where do we locate our nice new red barbecue truck? How about in our driveway, as Patrick and Lisa Brooks did? That might be a sketchy idea if your driveway is off the beaten path, but a darn good one if it's on Church Street, across from the Chincoteague Cultural Alliance and the twice-weekly Farmers and Artisans Market. It's an old-fashioned crushed-shell driveway, too, with room for a couple of umbrella tables for waiting or eating.

Backyard has a really good menu, with as much variety as a barbecue place can offer: pulled pork and chicken, ribs, beef brisket, and smoked wings, plus a couple of really interesting specialty sandwiches. All the traditional sides are there: baked beans, slaw, fries, mac and cheese, and cornbread, along with boiled baby red salt potatoes. This is good food, folks. The place is four years old, but we just discovered it this year. We've been able to try only a few things, including the brisket. I'm for it—but I'm a brisket guy. That's what we tend to make on our pellet smoker when it's not Thanksgiving. Backyard sells a lot of brisket. No surprise there.

✦ Backyard Firepit: 6312 Church Street, Chincoteague, VA 23336 (757) 336-7060 https://backyardfirepitbbq.com/ Email: backyardfirepit@icloud.com

HAVING A MELTDOWN

New on the Island for 2021, this food truck on Chicken City Road, just off Maddox near Black Narrows Brewery, is getting good reviews for big, cheesy, delicious comfort-food sandwiches. We look forward to trying it next time around. Your favorite review sites will no doubt collect many opinions quickly. So far, so good!

 ♦ Having a Meltdown: 6312 Church Street, Chincoteague, VA 23336 (757) 894-1650 https://www.chincoteaguechamber.com/directory/having-a-meltdown/ Email: gourmetgrilledcheese@yahoo.com

ISLAND DAWG

The space next to Woody's has been home to several food-truck enterprises. New for 2021 is this how-many-ways-can-you-make-a-hot-dog venture. So far, about eight ways, plus an assortment of tater tot meals. It's the first of its kind for the Island. There were no reviews when this guide was written, but check online as you read this!

 ♦ Island Dawg: 6700 Maddox Boulevard, Chincoteague, VA 23336

▪ COOK-IT-YOURSELF AND TAKEOUT ▪

Among the advantages of the food scene on Chincoteague is that almost everything is available as takeout. It's part of the restaurant culture: many visitors rent homes for groups large and small and ferry their meal home rather than sitting down to dine. Some places are take-out only, with a limited number of outdoor tables on site. It's a win-win.

If you're a good cook, or aspire to be, and would like to try your hand at preparing the finest and freshest American seafood and shellfish, you've reached nirvana on Chincoteague.

Those ingredients are available in many locales if you have a very good local supermarket or fish market. I can buy barrier island oysters in Northeast Pennsylvania and shuck them right at home. Maryland and Louisiana crab meat, backfin and jumbo lump, sits in the cooler an arm's reach from those oysters. Still, Island seafood goes to 11. You'll know that when you serve it. The variety is tremendous, the quality and freshness amazing. And, for the cherry on the sundae, the cost is substantially lower—as you'd expect. My mouth waters when I gaze into the refrigerated cases of local purveyors. Here are a few:

TIPPING FOR TAKEOUT: PLEASE!

We tip for takeout. That's a personal choice, but it's been tough recently for folks in the hospitality business. They have a short season to earn income. Takeout is a good value. A couple of extra bucks doesn't hurt, does it? God will repay you.

CAPTAIN ZACK'S: OUR GO-TO

Captain Zack's, corner of Maddox Boulevard and Deep Hole Road, may be the King of All Seafood Places. By all means, read reviews and make your choice, but Zack's is our default.

We have a long trip to the Island. Six of us used to arrive in one car. Now that we are grown, nine of us, one very small, arrive in five cars from several corners of the mid-Atlantic. Whoever hits the ground first brings dinner from Captain Zack's. The rest can collapse with a beer and revive ourselves with nourishment for body and soul unobtainable elsewhere. I don't mean to say other places aren't good. Other places are good. They just aren't Captain Zack's.

If not for the lime-green and Bimini-blue paint job and the brand-new-for-2021 miniature lighthouse and the full-sized anchor in the lot (come to think of it, that's plenty of advertising, right there), you might not notice Captain Zack's. It's a low, square, cinder-block building with the bare minimum of windows and doors. The magic happens inside. It's incredibly hot and steamy. How the staff survives is beyond me. They are overwhelmed with orders at busy times (much of the time, actually). Yet, in many, many years, no one at Captain Zack's has ever been anything but thoroughly kind to me. They've served up oysters, crab cakes, clam strips, flounder, shrimp, and all the other goodies, with loads of hush puppies, baked beans, buttered corn, coleslaw, green beans, and (of course) French fries, with a smile and sigh of relief that they got 'r' dun right once again. Lord love people who do what they do so well and gracefully.

You might think prices would be high, on account of all this. They aren't. You'll spend $20 each, maybe $25, and you won't regret it. Athletes like to say, "I left it all on the field." Zack's leaves it all in the takeout container.

Leaving Chincoteague is a sad time for us, for many reasons—these days, because our family must go our separate ways, for at least a while. We ordered an oyster fritter once on our way home from the island. A meal from Zack's for the road is a fine way to prolong the joy. Heaven on a bun. But I must admit I could not finish that fritter. You try, OK? For me. God bless.

♦ Captain Zack's: 4422 Deep Hole Road, Chincoteague, VA 23336
   (757) 336-3788 and (757) 336-7356 https://www.captzackseafood.com/
   Email: captzackseafood@gmail.com

RICKY'S SEAFOOD AND PRODUCE MARKET

Ricky's is a family-operated place a little down-island, not far off Main Street on Beebe Road. They'll steam or fry whatever they have for you to take home. In 2017 we had a crab feast to die for, laden with Old Bay, packed in a cardboard box, as it should be. This is the real thing; you'll remember it. I first tasted a Maryland crab feast with my Aunt Vivian in Pope's Creek, Maryland, on the water, served on butcher paper, with Miller draft beer, in the mid-1970s. You can't fake that. Crabs are hit-and-miss the last couple of years—call ahead or stop by. You'll find other things you like excellent produce in season, local jams, pickles, and relish. Wooden crab mallets. Island things. I like to hang out at Ricky's for a few minutes. It's a good place.

♦ Ricky's Seafood and Produce: 7432 Beebe Road, Chincoteague, VA 23336
   (757) 336-6867 https://www.chincoteague.com/rickys-seafood/

GARY HOWARD SEAFOOD

You know some places aren't designed around the tourist trade the moment you walk in. Gary Howard is one. A tiny place on Deep Hole Road where it curves towards Little Oyster Bay, there's room for maybe three cars on the oyster-shell lot. Not to worry. It won't take long to carry out your mission. Oysters to shuck. Pints of shucked oysters (not easy to find—here and Tom's Cove Aqua Farms are your best bets). Clams. Crabmeat, jumbo lump and backfin, for your best crab cakes, with Gary's private label, in a plastic take-out container. And fish—all kinds. You don't know what he's got until you get there, but I've never been disappointed. They'll steam anything for you, as a meal to take home.

Keep in mind, though, this is not a restaurant. It's an excellent sea-food market. We needed to be out doing things for a while after buying oysters this year, so the counter person put the sack of oysters in a plastic bag, dumped a scoop of ice on it, and tied it shut. Good people. I also met Gary himself for the first time. He emerged from the back in rubber boots and a T-shirt, a smile on his face when I greeted him. I'm pretty sure he works hard back there.

♦ Gary Howard Seafood: 5315 Deep Hole Road, Chincoteague, VA 23336 (757) 336-5178 (Does Gary have an online presence? I can't find it. Just go there, analog-style.)

RAY'S SHANTY: RESTAURANT AND SEAFOOD MARKET

I'd love to include a review of Ray's Shanty. I tried. I drove past the place for years, not realizing it was a restaurant. Most places feature a good amount of glass and a substantial entranceway, in addition to attention-getting signage. Not Ray's. They have a nice big sign, all right, with a pink polymer shrimp and moveable letters that tell you the daily menu features. If you miss the sign, though, the big, dark-green two-story building doesn't fit the restaurant mold. One single door allows guests into the restaurant side, on the west, and another into the seafood market side, on the east. I have to admit I didn't make the connection at first. Ray's has been run by its founders since1986. The more I heard locals and visitors sing Ray's praises on social media, the more I resolved to go. "Fantastic seafood," they said. "Good prices. Good portions. And friendly service!" What more can you ask? We set out on a Tuesday night during our stay in Chincoteague this year—one of the few times we've ventured off-island, other than to Wallops Flight Facility. Just our luck: two-hour wait. We bagged it.

The wait wasn't because of short staffing. The place was packed. From the vibe, it seemed the crowd was local. Waitresses were hustling big trays of food to the wood-paneled dining room, full of people enjoying themselves thoroughly. Three staff were managing arrivals and departures at the front counter. I wish I could provide a first-hand review. (Next year!) As far as I can tell, word-of-mouth is reliable. Go early.

My wife and I drove from New England to Florida in 1977. We took along Jane and Michael Stern's *Roadfood*, a book published long before the Internet led travelers to local restaurants off the beaten path. Among them was Archie's Seafood on Route 17 in Darien, Georgia, where we ate all the shrimp we could handle in view of the boats that brought them in. The local Toyota dealer had driven his Celica there for lunch, too.

Archie's was the most local of local places. It closed in 2006. Others are still open. Let's go while we can.

- Ray's Shanty: PO Box 13, 32157 Chincoteague Road, Wattsville, VA 23483 (757) 824-3429 http://www.raysshanty.com/ Email: Ray-Laura@RaysShanty.com

WHITERAVEN'S NEST

A few years ago, Whiteraven's nest was an interesting-looking produce store off Route 175 on the way to the Island. We always wanted to stop—but most people are hesitant to stop when that close to the Island on the first day of a vacation. Luckily for us, they relocated to Maddox Boulevard. Whiteraven is a three-sided structure, open on the front, with freezers, coolers, and a counter under the roof. It bills itself as a farmers market with a permanent seasonal location. That works for me. They specialize in fresh organic produce, including herbs, locally made preserves, salsa, pickles, and sauces, and locally sourced organic meats, which you buy frozen. Everything we've had is very good. You'll also find coffee, eggs, milk, Island honey, and desserts, including the elusive Smith Island cake (a regional legend) and a good assortment of seafood. If you're planning a special dinner, this is a great place to visit for the fixings—especially if you're grilling. Among the attractions are their two goats, Crimson and Clover, whom you can visit. This year, they had some kids. Kids love kids.

- Whiteraven's Nest: 6382 Maddox Boulevard, Chincoteague, VA 23336 (757) 894-4664 https://whiteravensnest.com/ Email: info@whiteravensnest.com

SEABEST

Seabest is in a garage, so you might miss it, but please don't. If you park on the right-hand side of the Island Foods supermarket on Cleveland Street, you can stroll over to Seabest. These are very nice people. They've got oysters, chicken necks for baiting crabs, oyster mallets for about $3, and small containers of Old Bay, along with daily offerings of fresh fish. We've done well there. You may get called "honey." Prepare yourself.

- Seabest Seafood: 6299 Cleveland Street, Chincoteague, VA 23336 (757) 336-5453 (Can't find them online. Just hop over the shrubs and go in.)

SALTS SEAFOOD

Salts is a new venture, among several exciting ones on the Island. When Black Narrows Brewery debuted in 2018, craft beer fans rejoiced: the Island finally had a key piece of the puzzle, missing to date. Good beer is good beer, and we enjoyed the fresh, innovative, locally sourced offerings of Black Narrows. Among its few shortcomings was the limited food menu (pretzels, brats, etc.—all good). Beer and oysters (among other seafood) are natural companions. In 2021, Black Narrows, housed in a former oyster-packing house, remodeled a seafood purveyor on an adjoining lot, turning it into Salts Seafood. The match was made in heaven.

You'll find oysters, shucked or steamed, Chincoteague clams, steamed shrimp, and crabs, including soft-shells when available (what more did you need?). Among the most popular offerings is the "oyster flight," something only a craft brewer, accustomed to beer flights, would think of. Imagine a half-dozen different varieties of oysters harvested from Tangier to Cape Charles for $12. Better imagine another one, right after that one. This is brilliance. You'll learn why Chincoteague oysters are called "salts" when you read the PPM of salt in each kind, like the IBUs in an India Pale Ale. Island oysters double the lesser varieties. Who knew?

You can carry your order from Salts Seafood next door to the brewery. You get it, right?

Keep up the great work, Black Narrows.

♦ Salts Seafood: 4522 Chicken City Road, Chincoteague, VA 23336
  (757) 336-7001 https://www.saltsseafood.com/
  Email: info@saltsseafood.com

TOM'S COVE AQUA FARMS

You will not believe the oysters at Tom's Cove. Chincoteague has always been known for oysters. Outside of the famous wild ponies, oysters are its best-known living creature. A hundred years ago, oysters were among the most popular foods on tables, humble and elaborate. They graced the menu in every swanky restaurant. Chincoteague shipped its wares in barrels, cans, and on ice, far and wide. Oyster fans all have their preferences, but Chincoteague Salts rate high. Always did.

The days of watermen working the wild oyster beds with long, heavy tongs have ended. Today, Chincoteague oysters are farmed: the "spat," or small oyster larvae, are placed carefully in the perfect spots, protected by metal-mesh cages, to grow and mature into the bivalves we love. It takes a year or two, maybe more—quite a while.

I've enjoyed every oyster I've ever had on Chincoteague. The very best came from Tommy Clark's Tom's Cove Aqua Farms on Lighthouse Lane, off Ridge Road on the east side of the Island. They're much larger and as delicious as a Chincoteague oyster can be.

Tom's Cove displays their wares at the Farmers and Artisans Market at the Chincoteague Cultural Alliance on Church Street, held Wednesdays and Saturdays. That's where I discovered them. You probably have to be on the Island to buy them for $6 a dozen—with shucked pints (30 or so, suitable for frying, stew, or fritters) at $17. We bought a dozen the first time around. Once we shucked and sampled them, we had to have more. Fortunately, the Aqua Farms are open six days a week during business hours. Lighthouse Lane is easily missed. Once you turn, keep going until you see piles of oyster shells. You've found Tom's Cove.

There's no storefront. You may not see people around. Someone will appear shortly, probably not because you're there. Tell them how many you want. Give them currency. They'll be back in a few minutes with your heaven-sent oysters. That's the best transaction you'll make all week.

✦ Tom's Cove Aqua Farms: 4522 Chicken City Road, Chincoteague, VA 23336 (757) 336-1945 https://www.tomscove.net/
Email: sales@tomscove.net

▪ BAKED GOODS AND ICE CREAM ▪
ON CHINCOTEAGUE

CHURCH STREET PRODUCE

I first visited Paula and Jerry Alm's Church Street Produce some years ago when shopping for crab cake ingredients. An authentic Maryland crab cake has few, other than crab: egg, mayonnaise (preferably Duke's, in our house), Old Bay, mustard, Worcestershire sauce, minimal breadcrumbs, or plain white bread (I've gravitated to bread), and fresh Italian parsley. At Island Foods that year, Italian parsley was notably absent. Heading up Church Street, contemplating crab cakes without the necessary dark-green flecks of parsley, I made a quick turn into the unpaved lot of Church Street Produce. It's a cool old building with some attention-getting stuff outside, including a tall lifeguard's chair. A vintage wooden screen door leads you inside, where you're welcomed by a limited but mouth-watering selection of the most gorgeous peaches, corn, and vegetables you've ever seen.

I didn't see any parsley—but as soon as she heard my story, Paula headed to the garden with a pair of scissors. She came back with a hefty bunch of the freshest Italian parsley possible. "That enough?" she asked. I liked Church Street right away.

A couple of years later, we heard about Tomato Pies. Church Street was baking peach and berry dessert pies and their special deep-dish tomato pie. It's nothing like pizza. It's also not like old-school Philadelphia tomato pies, in a category of their own, perhaps familiar only to Philadelphians. (I think of them as a pizza without cheese, not really a pizza at all, but well-loved in Philly). The Church Street tomato pie is more of a southern thing, a savory tomato blend, with chunks of the well-ripened vegetable baked in a toothsome crust. It can serve as lunch, dinner, or conceivably, breakfast. They are very good, as are the traditional dessert pies. Paula bakes every day, in season. The building flies a flag emblazoned with a tomato and the mathematical symbol pi. The pies have gained notoriety. Early on, people just bought them off the counter. Those days are gone. You might score a pie that wasn't spoken for, but the odds aren't that great. Call ahead. The earlier, the better, and order for later that day. Paula will text you when it's done. She'll also text you if you don't show up when you said you would. Hungry people are waiting for that pie. Get over there.

Which pie is best, you ask? Which sunny Saturday in May is best? Which walk-off home run is best? Why are you even *thinking* about this? Order some pies. Then decide.

♦ Church Street Produce: 6493 Church Street, Chincoteague, VA 23336 (757) 990-0463 https://www.chincoteague.com/ChurchStreetProduce/

ISLAND VOICES

JERRY AND PAULA ALMS, CHURCH STREET PRODUCE

In 1988, Jerry Alms never imagined he'd make over 3,000 pie crusts one summer, somewhere down the road. "I bought an old building, a former truck and boat repair garage, and started a woodworking shop there," Jerry told me. Then I met Paula." Paula, his wife-to-be, was an English teacher in Accomack schools (She retired in 2020 after 34 years). They made the Island their home. Jerry built up his woodworking business, making cabinets and furniture and refinishing old wood floors. Life was good.

Fast-forward to 2008. Paula's Uncle Brad had an idea: there was a demand for really good fresh produce. Why not put up a tent in the parking lot of the woodworking shop? It sounded good. Paula and Jerry bought 500 ears of corn. They hadn't done any advertising, and nobody knew they were in the produce business, off the beaten path on Church Street. It turned out to be a whole lot more corn than they needed.

Jerry and Paula Alms, Church Street Produce.

As time passed, they got better at it. "I can tick off on my fingers the things people really love," said Paula. "Corn, tomatoes, peaches, lopes, and watermelon." In season, you'll find gorgeous examples of all those. They grew herbs in their garden.

In 2010, they had another idea. Jerry's mom was a talented baker, and he was an outstanding piemaker himself. Paula's sister served them a southern-style tomato pie. They tried others at a farmers market and a restaurant. Before they knew it, they were in the pie business, using organic blueberries, strawberries, and a triple-berry mix, along with a cheesy tomato pie, all baked into Jerry's homemade crusts.

"We found equipment everywhere you can imagine," Paula said. "Restaurants that had gone out of business, secondhand things. We pieced it together. Mayor Leonard brought us chalkboards from the long-gone old elementary school. That's where we wrote our menu."

Church Street now makes 20 dessert pies of seven different kinds, along with tomato pies, every day, mostly to order. The three original berry fillings are joined by sour cherry, cherry berry, pecan, and chocolate pecan. What Paula likes to call "The Elusive Peach Pie," a more labor-intensive recipe, usually comes around only about once a week. Brownies and frozen chocolate-chip dough balls have been added to the lineup, too. The total for the 2021 season, May through September, was 3700. Jerry still made most of the crusts. And by the way—temperatures in the shop regularly hit 100 degrees.

The biggest problem Church Street faces is how to get everyone a pie, even with three double ovens in operation. "We have the most lovely customers," said Paula. "They're patient and kind. We try to bake enough for orders and walk-ins in if we can. If you're here for the week, we'll get you a pie." Most days, you'd have to be pretty lucky to walk in and find one on the counter. Just call in the morning, or stop in, and they'll text you when your pie is ready.

In the meantime, Jerry advised visitors to take one of the many boat tours run by Island captains. "In the '80s, a lot of people were coming mainly for the fishing," he observed. "Now, it's more families who appreciate the natural environment here." Paula agreed. "It's a different vibe on the Island. You're able to leave the attitude of the city behind. The people and businesses here operate a little differently. Once you learn how they work, you'll enjoy it."

· THE GREAT ICE CREAM DEBATE: ·
ISLAND CREAMERY VS. MR. WHIPPY'S

ISLAND CREAMERY

Do you like ice cream? Sorry. Bad joke. (Lactose-intolerant folks, we get it. Didn't mean you.) The important question is how good your ice cream has been. You may follow sites naming "the best ice cream in all fifty states." You may have sampled truly great ice cream such as (according to one of those sites) Milkcraft in West Hartford, Lappert's in Honolulu, Antney's Ice Cream in Pittsburgh, or . . . wait for it . . . Island Creamery, in Chincoteague, Virginia. More than one website has crowned it best in the state. Good reason, too.

First, it's exceptional ice cream. One taste will tell you that. Second, their imagination in the flavor arena is wide-ranging. Java Jolt, Snickers Cheesecake, and Bourbon Caramel Crunch lead the creativity parade. That said, more traditional offerings (Is any of this "traditional?") such as Pony Tracks and Marsh Mud (the signature flavor if there ever was one—this dark-chocolate masterpiece looks EXACTLY like marsh mud) have been wildly popular for years. Third, the savory handmade waffle cones and hand-dipped scoops are served up by a smiling local team who never seem to wilt, despite perpetually long lines. Don't despair—they move things along. The line will go faster than you think. They've studied the problem (a very good one to have), then addressed it with the intensity of a Chik-Fil-A, recently adding people to take your order as you wait so that the scoopers can devote themselves to scooping.

The Creamery has been building its reputation since 1975. They do one thing and do it very well. They used to make outstanding fudge that we brought home routinely but wisely decided to abandon the labor-intensive confection to focus on what they do best. The lines are there for a reason.

The Conklins, an old Island family, are ice cream royalty. Son Drew is managing the shop in Berlin, Maryland. There's another in Salisbury—but you're headed to Chincoteague, home of the original. Our granddaughter expressed her joy the first night the foraging party brought some home: "Ice cream cone! Ice cream cone!" The party went out nearly every night, always returning successfully. Some waits were longer than others, but never did anyone declare the effort too great. We had Island Creamery. Any questions?

◆ Island Creamery: 6243 Maddox Boulevard, Chincoteague, VA 23336
(757) 336-6236 https://www.islandcreamery.net/
Email: info@islandcreamery.net

MR. WHIPPY'S

We didn't visit Mr. Whippy's for years because we were Island Creamery people. On some issues, you simply have to take a stand. In Northeast Pennsylvania, where we're from, you're either a Penn State fan or a Notre Dame fan. If you say "neither," you don't count. So, it is with the two Chincoteague Ice Cream meccas, just one-tenth of a mile apart on Maddox Boulevard. Mr. Whippy's has been around over fifty years, Island Creamery forty-six. They're both outstanding local businesses with loyal followings. Many people assume they must be great rivals, but they're owned by first cousins, native to the Island, who get along just fine.

Here is the key question: do you like soft-serve ice cream or traditional ice cream? They're just different. Both have devoted fans. We like traditional ice cream, so we never went to Mr. Whippy's. Then Sugarbaker's closed.

Ah, Sugarbakers. Pull your chair up to the fire, lad, and let me tell you a story.

Sugarbakers was a tiny local bakery. Their donuts and breakfast pastries were much sought-after. I recall pedaling there pretty early (Island time) to get any sort of selection. If you waited too long, you were out of luck. The cinnamon rolls were to die for. The year after they closed, I made sure to bring stuff along to make our own cinnamon rolls. They were very good, too.

I've heard the building has issues. I don't know. In any case, it's unoccupied. Sugarbaker's ain't comin' back. That's what led us to Mr. Whippy's and their doughnuts. Turns out they are outstanding. If you enjoy doughnuts—and who doesn't—you'll like them. You can't NOT like them. They remind me of Sugarbaker's. The coffee is very good, too, beloved by locals.

I don't pretend Sugarbaker's was bakery nirvana. The place was incredibly tiny. The A/C couldn't keep up. The staff was overwhelmed. No matter how early you managed to wake up (on your vacation, yet) to make the bakery run, they were usually out of many things. The magic was being the hero when you scored good stuff for everyone. It was an Island Thing—but it's over, sadly. We seek alternatives.

When there's a rocket launch at Wallop's Island (pretty frequently), Mr. Whippy's makes themed doughnuts. The icing carries the theme: usually stratosphere blue, with shooting stars. You gotta love that. And if you also love soft-serve ice cream, all your bases are covered.

◆ Mr. Whippy's: 6201 Maddox Boulevard, Chincoteague, VA 23336
(757) 336-5122 http://www.misterwhippy.com/
Email: softserve@misterwhippy.com

ISLAND VOICES
KELLY CONKLIN, ISLAND CREAMERY

Kelly Conklin remembers the phone calls coming in. It was April of 2014. Virginia newspapers and TV stations. Then national media—*The Times*, *Fox News*. Before it was over, there were calls from places like Lithuania. Kelly told me the story: "TripAdvisor had just named the top 10 places in the US for ice cream, and we were #1. They didn't give us any warning or anything. They just published it. We got some very big publicity not long before that when the food editor for the *Virginian-Pilot* published a feature called "30 Places to Eat in Virginia before You Die." We were number one in that, too, alongside some pretty high-end places, but the TripAdvisor rating got around. Most of the people we serve are coming to the Island anyway, but we do meet our share of folks who've made a special trip just to taste our ice cream."

Pretty good for a place that started in a pool hall. Or rather, started *as* a pool hall.

"My mother and father, Nancy and Bob, bought three lots here on Maddox Boulevard in 1965 for less than $5000," Kelly related. "This was shortly after the Ash Wednesday storm that devastated the Island. They weren't sure at first what sort of business they wanted to put there. They moved an old building onto the site. It used to be a pool hall. In fact, my grandfather managed that pool hall in the 1940s. So, there was quite a connection. Ocean City had a candy kitchen. They decided to start one, too. They added Breyer's ice cream in the 1970s, about the time Mueller's opened downtown as an ice cream parlor." Kelly and his wife were both teachers. In 1985, he got some further education that would change his life. "The most popular school for learning the creamery trade was at Penn State University. Ben and Jerry took the correspondence course. I took the intensive on-campus course. We made the decision to make Island Creamery ice cream ourselves, right here. We still do. One hundred percent."

Did the Conklin family imagine Island Creamery would be named best in the nation? "I never set out to do anything like that," said Kelly. "I always wanted to make the best ice cream I could make. It's so subjective. I travel a lot and always look at what other people are doing. I steal every good idea I can. If they're doing a better job than I am, I want to know why."

One of the big issues now is the lines. When we stay on Chincoteague, we often send out a foraging party to bring home the ice cream while the rest of

Kelly Conklin, Island Creamery.

us relax. They text with news about how far the line stretches up Maddox. "We've always put a lot of effort in the speed of service," Kelly told me. "During COVID, when we had to count the number of customers in the store and minimize contact, we made the decision to replace the traditional cash register with a point-of-sale system using a tablet. Now each person has only one job to do. Of course, Chik-Fil-A is the gold standard at that. We wanted to handle the lines just as well. Our main concern was whether it would speed up service. Turns out it does speed it up, and it's more accurate, too."

And the secrets behind the "best in the US" ice cream? "Butterfat content is a big part of it," Kelly told me. "Legally, 10% butterfat is required for the label 'ice cream.' When we started, we went to fourteen percent because that was the highest we could go. Some of our flavors are seventeen percent now. Butterfat coats the tongue and gives the ice cream richness." And the choice of flavors? "We have room for only thirty-two at a time," noted Kelly. "I've seen gourmet chefs on TV create very exotic flavors that I'm sure are tasty but wouldn't interest most people. We like to be innovative and come up with a twist without being too trendy. We create seasonal flavors like pumpkin pie, apple cobbler, and apple cider sorbet in the fall, sugar cookie at Christmas, and red velvet and cinnamon at Valentine's Day. Our best seller is still vanilla, which we make with the best Madagascar vanilla extract we can find. You can't rush vanilla."

The second most popular flavor at the Creamery is our family's favorite: Marsh Mud. The story made Kelly Conklin chuckle. "Marsh Mud was a mistake," he recalled. "I made a batch of chocolate with more than double the amount of chocolate it was supposed to have. It looked like road tar. We didn't want to waste it, so we called it something—I don't remember what—and it sold well. We changed the name two or three times until we settled on 'Marsh Mud.'"

Cookie dough isn't far behind, in third place. "We make all our own cookie dough, brownie pieces, and fudge," Kelly told me. "'Adult' flavors like Bourbon Caramel Crunch, Limoncello, Rum Raisin, and Cherries Jubilee contain at least a smidge of the actual liquor, along with flavoring. Kelly got the idea from a New York restaurant he saw on the Food Channel making "adult milkshakes." "Sounded to me like it would make delicious ice cream," Kelly remembered. "You can't put too much alcohol in it, or it won't freeze well. We don't want our ice cream dripping all over."

More than one Island Creamery wasn't in the plans until recently, when opportunities arose in Berlin, Maryland, and Salisbury, Virginia, both at prime locations. "We'd love to see the next generation carry it on," said Kelly. "If we can't do something really well, we won't do it. The two new locations are working well. Right now, the issue is help. We need good employees. Our business has become more consistent year-round, as more people are staying on the Island in the off-season."

Kelly sees the benefit to everyone in the growth and development on Chincoteague. "The Island is a special place for so many people," he reflected. The waterpark and the sale of the campground were controversial when they were proposed. The park has turned out to be a nice addition. The drawback is that more visitors do create more traffic and longer wait times. Be sure you make reservations when you plan to dine out."

Kelly also advised taking a boat tour. "There are so many different kinds, depending on what you want," he advised. "To really see the Island, you have to see it by water."

Be prepared for the mosquitoes, but don't let them keep you away. You can deal with them if you time it right. Don't plan to be on the marsh at dusk. Learn about the beach and what you need to bring to enjoy yourself."

What might we find on the Island Creamery flavor list in the future? "Some of the new flavors have been really popular," said Kelly. The pineapple upside-down cake. Lucky Charms, which we make with what amounts to the milk from a bowl of cereal. For St. Patrick's Day, we have a Guinness flavor, with a chocolate and coffee profile. I've been thinking about an ice cream based on Paula Deen's Ooey Gooey Butter Cake. And it would be great to come up with something based on oysters. No oysters in it, but salty and briny. That might work. You could close your eyes and envision the oysters."

We'll be in the line for that.

ISLAND VOICES

DREW CONKLIN, ISLAND CREAMERY BERLIN AND SALISBURY

Drew Conklin is the third generation of his family to operate Island Creamery, but he doesn't even know how many generations they go back on Chincoteague. "I got my degree in History and Political Science from Salisbury University," Drew told me. "I'm sort of obsessed with history. My grandmother was born on Assateague. The Lloyds and Williams's in our family used to operate the lighthouse. Some are buried there. It's difficult to get permission to visit those graves now because they're part of the refuge. I worked at the Refuge for a while, so it was easier. Some of our ancestors go back to James Alone."

As you might expect, a young man whose family founded Island Creamery always kept busy. "We used to own Steamers. When I was seven or eight, I got two dollars an hour to pick up trash. I only worked about an hour a week. I figured that one out pretty fast. By ten or twelve, I was a dishwasher and a busboy. By thirteen, I was assistant ice cream maker. I scooped ice cream until I graduated from Chincoteague High School. Always, in the back of my head, I wanted to run my own store, to carry on what our family started. When I met my fiancée Jen at the Creamery, I saw that become real."

Today Drew and Jen operate two Island Creameries in Belin and Salisbury, Maryland. "We started Berlin in 2016 and Salisbury in 2018. We didn't do conventional advertising. My Dad always believed in donating to every group in our community—Little League, Big Brothers and Big Sisters. We followed that example. Knowing how many people went out of their way to visit the Chincoteague creamery, we thought it would take a while to get the new businesses going without that kind of following. But right from the start, they took off. People are loyal. Bless them."

"The first thing I realized was how much Dad does," Drew told me. "Most of our employees are young. It's often their first job. We want them to work in a safe environment in a family business and help them succeed. People think because it's ice cream, we must have a lot of fun, but it can get a little tense, especially with a drive-through. The shutdown of inside dining for a while, and the masks, took away a little of the friendliness. For some people, a drive-through ice cream cone became one of their few escapes. I never cease to be amazed by how people stand in line in Chincoteague. They don't complain. I didn't understand that as a kid. Now, I do. They're going for ice cream, so they're not in a bad mood. Even if they are, it'll get a lot better very soon."

It's tough to get a new flavor on the list at Island Creamery. "I talked about Peanut Butter and Jelly for years. It's complicated to make—but it's been a hit. I'd like to try flavors based on favorite breakfast cereals. And S'mores. Really simple but worth doing. At Bojangles, they serve a blueberry muffin with cinnamon glaze. That would make great ice cream." Exotic ideas don't have the same appeal. "People suggest Old Bay or oyster ice cream. I respectfully request to be excluded from that project."

· WHERE'S THE BREAD? ·

The South isn't known for bread one way or the other. Biscuits, pancakes, grits, yes. Bread, no. Italian and French bread are famous for good reason, but they don't play much of a role in Virginia cookery. Though good bread in that tradition (crusty, chewy, and full of welcome cavities:

a baguette or ciabatta) would be a fine accompaniment to any Chincoteague meal, you'll seldom find it. Poseidon's Pantry on Maddox Boulevard has a creditable baguette, as you would find at a good bakery (along with many other good hard-to-find things). That's your best bet if you're a bread lover. Island Foods carries the "supermarket version," but the crust is sorely lacking. Sea Star makes its sandwiches on outstanding bread but doesn't sell it by the loaf. Bread is not why you traveled to Chincoteague, right? On the bright side, you can find country ham (see the feature on country ham).

· BLACK NARROWS BREWING ·

Among the things Chincoteague needed to become perfect was a brewery and brewpub. In 2018, one arrived. Black Narrows, named after the area of the channel closest to Chincoteague, opened its doors just in time for New Year's, with the old swing bridge as its logo. Josh and Jenna Chapman, and Jenna's parents Bob and Wendy Huntley, dreamed it, built it, and run it with family. By the end of 2018, they were named Virginia's Brewery of the Year. Even they were surprised—though perhaps they shouldn't have been. They're brewing a wide variety of really good beer in a taproom environment beautifully converted from a run-down oyster shucking house that says, "Welcome home." The barley, the wheat, most of the hops, the sometimes-exotic herbs and flowers used in the brews, and even a strain of natural yeast, are sourced from Virginia, close to the Island. Oysters themselves have actually contributed to the beer.

Visitors to the taproom can enjoy a draft inside or under a big tent outside at traditional German beer-garden-style tables. Lagers, ales, an IPA, a tart ale, and a wheat beer have found their way to the taps over time. Crowlers and growlers are on hand, too, for taking home to a crab feast. Originally, the taproom offered only giant soft pretzels, brats, and hot dogs as accompaniments to the brews. Now, a new affiliated business on the same lot expands the possibilities for diners. (See Salts Seafood)

✦ Black Narrows Brewing: 4522 Chicken City Road, Chincoteague, VA 23336 (757) 336-7001 https://blacknarrowsbrewing.com/
  Email: info@blacknarrowsbrewing.com

Wine can be found all over the Island. Let us give thanks. Virginia is a state with many excellent wineries. Some are represented at the small but pleasant Virginia ABC (Alcohol Board of Control) store just off Maddox Boulevard near the H & H Pharmacy. The ABC is the only place you can buy distilled spirits. You can find a passable section of wine at Island Foods, the Atlantic Shoals Surf Shop on the traffic circle on Maddox Boulevard, and a couple of convenience stores.

Wine, Coffee, and Gourmet, in the downtown shopping district on Main Street, keeps a large and well-chosen assortment on hand for people who take their choice of wine seriously. They claim a thousand different bottles (and 100 craft beers to boot, along with—bless their hearts—premium cigars). This is a place with a mission.

Poseidon's Pantry, a small gourmet shop on Maddox Boulevard with very good things to eat and drink (and excellent sandwiches), keeps good wine (and Belgian beer!) on the shelves as well.

♦ Wine Coffee and Gourmet: 4103 Main Street, Chincoteague, VA, 23336 (757) 336-2610 https://www.chincoteaguechamber.com/directory/wine-cheese-more/ Email: islandbutterfly26@yahoo.com

♦ Poseidon's Pantry: 6219 Maddox Boulevard, Chincoteague, VA, 23336 (757) 336-6666 http://www.poseidonspantry.com/ Email: info@poseidonspantry.com

· THE CAFFEINE SCENE ·

MAIN ST. SHOP AND COFFEEHOUSE

I am not a coffee drinker. (Can you believe it?) I drink coffee on special occasions with others who enjoy it. For those occasions, a coffee shop is the right venue. You can get coffee at many places on Chincoteague (McDonald's, if you like). Two places stand out for relaxed, hospitable coffee: Main Street Shop and Coffeehouse, and Amarin.

Once upon a time, the old steel "swing bridge" led visitors into Chincoteague via Main Street. In 2010 the new causeway bridge was completed, ending at a light on Main Street. Across Main Street is the Main Street Shop and Coffeehouse. It's a good place. The shop takes up both floors of a former residence. As many reviewers have noted online, it's far more "shop" than "coffeehouse." Closed altogether because of the pandemic in 2020, it opened for 2021 serving beverages only, absent the pastries of previous years, with shaded outdoor seating only. It's among our favorite places to browse, shop, and converse.

Yes, the coffee is good (milk alternatives are available). The main attraction is the well-curated selection of clothing, housewares, linens, books, and giftware. The dishes, glassware, tablecloths, teakettles, and whatnot are a delight for the eyes. I've never left without something that takes me back to the Island whenever I use it.

+ Main Street Shop and Coffeehouse: 4288 Main Street, Chincoteague, VA 23336 (757) 990-2207 http://www.art-plus-life.com/ Email: info@mainstreet-shop.com

AMARIN

Amarin was a bit of a game-changer on the Island. The shop opened in 2019. I recall vividly the Facebook photos of their brand-new croissant machine being installed. Homemade croissants? On Chincoteague? This was new. Amarin Coffee is a brand of Arabica coffee grown in the central highlands of Vietnam, launched in the U.S. in 2019. Amazingly—or perhaps not—the first Amarin store in the U.S. opened on the Island, on Maddox Boulevard close to Main Street. I'd love to have sat in on the meeting where the first location was chosen.

I could tell from her posts that Yen Nguyen, the Woman in Charge, was a dynamo who would make it work no matter what. She did. Both drive-through and table service are available. The shop is simple, comfortable, and spotless. We had coffee, shrimp spring rolls, and banh mi sandwiches the first season, all delicious.

They remained open during 2020 "COVID season" and returned full swing in 2021, complete with souvenir cloth masks "for everyone to mark ended of crazy pandemic." (The English was not perfect, but the thought surely was.) Sadly, the banh mi sandwiches were absent, but the shrimp (or vegetarian) spring rolls were as good as before. They come three to an order. I defy you to eat three.

As for the croissants: I'm guessing you've never had croissants like these. I've eaten my share of croissants. The supermarket versions are usually unworthy of the name. Even good croissants are often golden-brown, light-hearted, and squishy. Amarin's are bold, brown, and crispy, of substantial crust and filled with interior caverns that could house small bears. Yes, they're soft when you pull them apart, but there's a French character to the exterior. Amarin offers chocolate, almond, and coconut, all very good. Nothing can beat the "butter croissants," as they're listed on the menu. Get there early. You're not alone in your quest for these croissants.

When you visit Amarin, you will undoubtedly see Yen Nguyen, the Woman in Charge, presiding over the kitchen and ensuring that things go well. To her, we say, Brava!

♦ Amarin: 6141 Maddox Boulevard, Chincoteague, VA 23336
(757) 336-7229 https://www.amarincoffeeusa.com/
Email: info@amerincoffeeusa.com

▪ *2021 REVIEWS ▪

We visited the Island in the pandemic year of 2020 and found most everything open, with masks. We enjoyed the trip thoroughly. Things were even better in 2021, with one new twist: most places, even small ones, were short-staffed. Restaurants and hotels had the greatest difficulty. Signs asked visitors to be kind to employees who did show up. People just weren't working. Suffice it to say that many guests didn't have a good experience on occasion; the staff necessary to run businesses weren't available. Many restaurants closed on a rolling schedule. Wait times were often long. The takeaway: if you read a negative review of a hotel or restaurant dated 2020 or 2021 based on poor service, it's wise to take it with a grain of salt. That's usually a good thing in a saltwater environment.

HOW TO SHUCK AND EAT AN OYSTER

In 1870, 4.5 million lived in New York City. They ate a million oysters every day. Oysters were big business—the mainstay of the Chincoteague economy, then. Sets of China included an oyster plate. Every restaurant served oysters, often prepared a dozen ways. Today, as then, there is only one best way to eat an oyster: shuck it and eat it. You can add lemon. You probably should. Cocktail sauce? Sure. Spice it up with horseradish. It's all good. You're enjoying the oyster the way God intended, as the first brave human ever to eat an oyster did, with added embellishments—or not.

You can eat oysters in any month, whether or not it has an "R" in it. Long ago, oysters often came from warmer waters, sat out on docks for a while, and were shipped without the benefit of machine-made ice or refrigeration. The chances of a spoiled oyster went way up in the warmer months. That's also when oysters spawn. In many areas, the season was closed. Today, none of those issues stop you from enjoying oysters any time, especially when visiting Chincoteague.

What will you need? First, fresh oysters. On Chincoteague, that's the easy part. I've had excellent oysters from a half-dozen places. The local variety is delicious. They're also inexpensive on the island—$6 a dozen in 2021. You'll need an oyster knife, probably available for a few bucks from the same place you bought your oysters. Any number of stores sell them. If you're shopping in advance, OXO has a very good rubber-handled one for $11. My own is made by a company called Toadfish. The aqua-blue handle is secured to the polished blade with Allen screws. It sells for $38. I love it. That's how I am with oysters. Pay no attention. I'm setting a bad example.

You'll also need a non-slip surface to set the oyster on, like a polymer or wooden cutting board. Even after you wash the unshucked oysters thoroughly (which you should), they'll still make a mess on your cutting board. Then, you'll need an oven mitt (Plan on washing it after you've finished). The oven mitt protects the hand holding the oyster. Your dominant hand (left in my case, since I'm a lefty like Ned Flanders) holds the knife. If the knife slips on a stubborn shell, the oven mitt will protect your tender flesh. An oyster knife is not sharp like a paring knife, but it is ground to a thin edge and has a spear point. If the point slips and you stab yourself while not wearing an oven mitt, you'll notice. I've done it. Once. Now, I have an oven mitt. Some people will tell you to lay down a kitchen towel and cover your hand with it. These people undoubtedly experienced shuckers who have not stabbed themselves with an oyster knife. I say, oven mitt.

OK—ready to shuck. Your cutting board is on the counter. Your free hand is protected, your oyster knife in the other. Lay the oyster with the larger, rounded side down (the side you leave the meat in when you serve it) and the smaller, flat side up. At the back, the narrow end is a seam, or joint, where the oyster would hinge if you steamed it open. Insert the point of the oyster knife into that seam. Work it around until it finds a purchase—a little yielding spot where, with some pressure, the knife begins to find its way between the two shells. Wiggle the knife steadily and slowly back and forth, slightly up and down. The brittle shell may fragment slightly, producing some shrapnel. That's OK. Use more pressure—not so much the knife slips, mind you—until you feel the upper shell yielding. Pry it steadily upward a bit, then run the knife's blade around the perimeter of the shell, left and right, until it pops off. Don't tip the lower shell. The natural liquor is inside, with the meat.

Set the oyster on the platter that will soon make its way to the jubilant diners at the dinner table, discard the upper shell, and repeat with the next oyster. Do this until you're finished or tired. Then let someone else try. If you cannot get an oyster to open, set it aside. Come back to it after you've shucked the rest. Sometimes, it's easy on the second try, as if by magic. Why? Who knows? If you never can open it, forget about it. They're half a buck. These things happen.

Bob Weir of the Grateful Dead was asked in the 1980s if success had spoiled the band. "I was noticing the other night, for instance," Bobby said, "That when I'm going through pistachios—the hard-to-open ones, I don't bother with them anymore." So, it is with stubborn oysters. Don't go nuts.

The most memorable oyster I ever had was brought up from the channel by my daughter when she was 11. We were kayaking. Our guide had complimented us on what naturals our girls were. We crossed an oyster bed, and he pulled a few up. My daughter did, too. One of our companions had his knife and swiftly opened the oyster for us. My daughter had never eaten one. You have to prepare yourself the first time. She taste-tested it, wrinkled her nose, stuck out her tongue, and passed it to me. It was delicious.

She loves them now. This year, a decade and a half later, at a dinner where 8 of us surrounded a table laden with oysters and crab cakes, she reflected on what a luxury it was to be able to slurp down as many as you want. So true. Thank you, Lord, for this sweet, sweet life.

The world record for shucking oysters is 39 in 60 seconds. Those oysters were set up individually in a special wooden trough. Still, that's insane. Don't try this at home. Take your time, be safe, and enjoy it. It's not a race. Think about how good it will be to eat them.

Good shucking!

~∽~

Toadfish: https://toadfishoutfitters.com/
OXO Oyster Knife: https://www.oxo.com/oyster-knife.html

· YOU REALLY SHOULD KNOW ·
ABOUT COUNTRY HAM

Country ham is a little-known secret among Northerners. You may find one or two in stock at Island Foods on Chincoteague. If you're traveling from north of the Mason-Dixon Line and open to an American culinary adventure, consider bringing one home for a big meal later. Country hams are not like ordinary hams or "city hams." They aren't just "smoked hams" or so-called "Smithfield" hams (a brand name). The "quintessential dish of the South," they're smoked, dry-cured with salt, and hung to age. They keep dry and at room temperature, for several years. The process of cooking a country ham begins three days prior. The ham is soaked, and the water changed daily to remove the salt. Then it's boiled in a large pot until done. We've served them at Christmas since 2007.

They're the centerpiece of the meal. Thomas Jefferson served country ham at Monticello. You can, too.

You can buy a country ham online, direct from producers and retailers. On the Eastern Shore, they're a routine item and a much better value. Consider it. Next Christmas, when the family gathers, the meal that unites you will also be a memory of your time on Chincoteague. No T-shirt can do that, right? There's a country ham in our basement right now.

LOGISTICS

· ROUTES TO THE ISLAND: BY CAR ·

The Delmarva Peninsula is a long stretch of geography, extending 170 miles from southern Delaware to Cape Charles, VA, with the Chesapeake Bay on the west and the Delaware River, Delaware Bay, and the Atlantic Ocean on the east. The Chesapeake Bay is three to thirty miles wide, a marine estuary unmatched in the U.S. Untold numbers of rivers, streams, and creeks drain into it.

We love the Bay. The challenge is getting across it. Only two bridges make that possible if you're traveling to Chincoteague and Assateague from the West. The northern option is the "Bay Bridge," or Chesapeake Bay Bridge, officially the Governor William Preston Lane Jr. Memorial Bridge, part of route 50 from Annapolis, Maryland, to Kent Island, Maryland. It was built in 1952, with a dual span added in 1973. It's a long, tall bridge, challenging if you have difficulty with such bridges. The EZ pass toll is $2.00, levied eastbound only (if you aren't carrying an EZ Pass, you'll get a bill for $4.00). The southern alternative is the Chesapeake Bay Bridge Tunnel. Built in 1964, over 17 miles long, it's a marvel of engineering that both shortens your trip and inspires wonder. The EZ Pass toll is $14 to $18; the higher rate is in effect Friday to Sunday (beach days!). From the south, the Bay Bridge Tunnel is the way to go. From the north, use major highways, such as Route 95 from the north and northeast, then Route 1 (with tolls) through mid-Delaware, to Route 113, also good-sized. "Beach traffic" is normal on weekends in season. Some of the most popular U.S. beaches lie in Delaware, Maryland, and Virginia.

· ROUTES TO THE ISLAND: BY AIR ·

Yes, you can fly to Chincoteague. Salisbury, Maryland, or Salisbury/Ocean City, airport identifier SBY, is served by American and Piedmont Airlines.

It may be tricky to find connections. From Salisbury, you're just over an hour away. Five major rental agencies can set you up with a vehicle. You can also fly to Baltimore/Washington Airport (BWI) and drive to Chincoteague via the Bay Bridge, about three hours, not allowing for traffic. A similar strategy by way of Philadelphia (PHL) involves a three to four-hour drive as well, also not allowing for traffic. (Hint: there will be traffic.)

· HEALTH CARE ·

CALL 911 ON CHINCOTEAGUE IN A MEDICAL EMERGENCY. Chincoteague provides 24-hour Advanced Life Support services to residents and visitors. It maintains two ambulances. A staff of twelve National Registered Paramedics work from the Chincoteague Volunteer Fire Company on Deep Hole Road.

There's no hospital on the small Island of Chincoteague. Two are close: Riverside Shore Hospital in Onancock, Virginia, a 52-bed hospital, 19 of them critical care, is 34 miles away. Atlantic General in Berlin, Maryland, is a 62-bed hospital, six of them critical care, 50 miles from the Island.

For non-emergency care, including dental issues, The Eastern Shore Rural Health System maintains the Chincoteague Island Community Health Center at 4049 Main Street, open 8 AM to 6:30 PM during the week and on Saturdays seasonally. Call them at 757-336-3682.

· DENTISTS ·

Two dentists, Morrison Dental and Island Dental, have offices on Chincoteague, very close to each other on Main Street.

· CLOSEST OFF-ISLAND RESOURCES: · POCOMOKE AND SALISBURY

Pocomoke, Maryland, is a town of about 4,000 people, 22 miles from Chincoteague, half an hour away. It will take half an hour or more to get almost anywhere of significance off the Island. Before the causeway was built, it took half an hour to get across the channel. So, maybe that's not so bad.

There's a Walmart Supercenter (a smaller version) and a Lowe's at the turn on Route 13 in Pocomoke. AutoZone and Advance Auto also have stores in Pocomoke.

If you can't find something you need on the island or in Pocomoke, you're probably headed to Salisbury, Maryland, the commercial center of the Delmarva Peninsula, 50 miles and about an hour from Chincoteague. I stayed in Salisbury while doing a book signing during Pony Penning on Chincoteague (a one-night stay on Chincoteague during Pony Penning is a pipe dream). During the drive to the Island, my daughter and I watched dark storm clouds descend on that year's Pony Penning, drenching the crowd. Driving in from Salisbury turned out to be a fine choice.

Salisbury boasts a Target and a Best Buy, among other resources. Locally owned businesses on the Island, in Pocomoke, or Salisbury may offer what you're seeking. I mention these national chains because they're easy to find and can often solve problems quickly.

· GROCERIES: ON-ISLAND OR OFF? ·

If you can't find a grocery item at Island Foods or one of the good specialty shops on the Island, visit Food Lion in Oak Hall on Route 13, not far away. We've shopped at Island Foods and its predecessors for almost 20 years. It's far better than it once was and reliable for our needs when staying on the Island. Yes, it's small. No, we wouldn't want to depend on it year-round. The aisles are narrow, and the selection, in some cases, is limited. Honestly, we've done well there. The beer and wine offerings are fine. Good cheese is on hand. Grillers will find what they need. Grey Poupon mustard? No problem. You'll also find specialty items local to the region, like breading for seafood. They have drugstore items, bug repellent and sunscreen, a good selection of water and drinks, a worthwhile produce aisle, and a deli counter.

♦ Island Foods: 6277 Cleveland Street, Chincoteague, VA 23336 (757) 336-5289 Email: islandfoodsgreatvalu@gmail.com

· WHAT TO BRING HIKING, BIRDING, · AND PONY WATCHING: BINOCULARS, GUIDES, AND BUG STUFF

If you're planning on walking nature trails, birdwatching, pony watching, or kayaking on Chincoteague or Assateague, the first thing to pack is insect repellent in quantity and variety. Bugs are a bigger annoyance in the Chincoteague National Wildlife Refuge on Assateague than in town.

Insect habitat is near-perfect there, and spraying isn't done, as it is in the town of Chincoteague.

At the end of the day, "repellent" means just that. A hungry mosquito or green-headed fly may be repelled but still bite. Many veteran birders can be seen on trails and roadsides in long pants, long sleeves, a big hat, and even an insect net over their heads. The best repellent is clothing the pests can't bite through.

You'll need a bird guide, such as one by Roger Tory Peterson (The classic. Mine was signed by the author in the early 1980s), David Sibley, Donald and Lillian Stokes, Ken Kaufman, or the *National Geographic*. As soon as you see a bird, your best bet is to take your guide out right away. You *think* you'll remember its field marks for later, but birds are different in subtle ways, including size, which are easily forgettable. Looking it up while you are looking up *at it* is the best plan.

While most guides feature color photos, Peterson, a master illustrator, hand-painted his birds with arrows pointing to the key field marks and descriptions on the facing page. I find his paintings much more helpful than photos. That's one of the reasons (along with a certain sentimental attachment) for my loyalty to Peterson guides. We gave our two-year-old granddaughter one for her second birthday. We figured she would put it aside for later in life, but she enjoys reading it like a very complex picture book and already knows about a dozen birds by sight, including "grackle."

We met Roger Tory Peterson informally once, at the Visitor's Center in Cape May State Park, New Jersey, at ten minutes to midnight, just before the teams from that year's World Series of Birding were due in. The World Series of Birding is a competition: teams of four head out in a car at midnight and return 24 hours later with a record of all the species they've heard and seen. Companies like Nikon and National Geographic sponsor teams. Peterson wasn't competing that year. He was there to see the final tally. We greeted him warmly and exchanged a few friendly words. A lovely man.

If you're interested in an odd thing, you can meet the biggest celebrities who do that thing. Peterson died in 1996, finally, we imagine, getting his own wings.

You can also buy a field guide to the ponies. One is published annually by Steve and Darcy Cole, who contributed photos to *The Traveler's Guide*. The CVFC is allowed by the Department of the Interior to maintain the herd at 150. All those ponies have names, histories, and, usually, distinctive coloration, patterns, or markings that allow identification at a distance. It's fun to learn the names of the ponies you're seeing. Some, like the stallion Riptide, are Island celebrities. The mahogany-brown, golden-maned pony is the lookalike of his father, Surfer Dude, "the most famous Chincoteague pony since Misty," who died of natural causes at age 23 in 2015.

Last, you'll need binoculars. If you can borrow a good pair for your trip to the Island, by all means, do. See how you like birding. You'll need them for pony-watching, too. Decades ago, the ponies were allowed up close, unfenced. Today, for safety, they're fenced off at some distance. Without binoculars, you'll see that ponies are out there, but you can't get a good view unless you're on a tour boat or in a kayak and are able to approach them closely.

If you can, avoid binoculars that are too big or too small. They'll be heavy and hard to keep steady if they are too big. If they're too small, they won't gather enough light to get a good view of birds. The small field of view will require you to shift them around to keep moving birds in sight.

You'll need enough magnification to see details. 8 x 42 or 10 x 42 (eight to ten times magnification, with a 42 mm objective lens, the larger end of the binocular) is the ideal size. 7-power will work but can be frustrating at longer distances. 25mm binoculars are too compact to perform well. 50 mm are very bright and take in a wide area but get heavy fast. We've tried the whole range. 8 x 42 or 10 x 42 is the sweet spot. They're often called "roof-prism" binoculars. They should be waterproof and durable enough to withstand dropping. Fortunately, the real cost of good binoculars has fallen. Serious birders often spend a small fortune, but that isn't necessary. A pair made by companies like Nikon or Celestron, or privately branded for companies like Cabela's or L.L. Bean, can be had for $100-500, with good offerings on the lower side. Chinese-made knockoffs sell for as little as $50. They won't be as sharp, fog proof, or durable but may work well for your trip to Chincoteague. Many families acquire several pairs over time—as you upgrade, the old ones become part of your optics arsenal.

Stow a microfiber cleaning cloth or two in your case. Taken from an air-conditioned home to a humid Chincoteague day, binoculars will fog up in seconds and keep fogging up until the glass warms a few minutes.

Also, a wide neoprene strap (a replacement for the chintzy webbing strap that comes standard) will make your binoculars far more comfortable in the field. Only about ten bucks, and so nice.

- ✦ Field Guide to the Ponies:
  https://www.poniesinthemist.com/booklets
- ✦ Roger Tory Peterson Field Guides:
  https://www.hmhbooks.com/peterson

▪ EQUIPMENT RENTALS: UMBRELLAS, ETC. ▪

Your trip to Chincoteague may require some bulky equipment: chairs, umbrellas, coolers, boogie boards, and beach wagons to carry it all onto the sand. If you're steaming seafood, you may need an oversized pot. All this takes up a lot of space in the family vehicle. You can buy those things on the Island—but then, how to get them home? Chincoteague Island Outfitters on Eastside Road rents all that stuff, in addition to the more widely available kayaks and beach bikes. Prices are on their website so you can make the buy/rent decision (check the cabinets in your rental for a steamer pot first—you'll often find one).

To their credit, Chincoteague Island Outfitters also carry the Toadfish line of crab-cracking tools and oyster knives—the very best. My Toadfish knife is a prized possession.

- ✦ Chincoteague Island Outfitters: 7885 Eastside Road, Chincoteague, VA 23336 (757) 336-5129 https://www.chincoteagueislandoutfitters.com
  Email: Cislandoutfitters@gmail.com

▪ CAR TROUBLE ▪

Two full-time locally owned auto repair shops are located on the Island, both easily found. Neither has weekend hours. Adams Auto Repair has a towing service. As you can imagine, most of their customers are their neighbors on the Island but don't hesitate to call if you need help with your vehicle while traveling. You'll find good reviews online from vacationers who were grateful for fast and capable assistance.

Auto repair shops get very busy and sometimes can't pick up the phone. If you don't get an answer during business hours, stop in. Neither shop is far from where you are.

- ✦ R Libertino Auto Repair: 4515 Chicken City Road, Chincoteague, VA 23336 (757) 336-3465 https://r-libertino-auto-repair.business.site/

- ✦ Adams Auto Repair (also towing): 5006 Deep Hole Road, Chincoteague, VA 23336 (757) 894-7206 https://www.facebook.com/adamsautorepair2015/

▪ RV TROUBLE ▪

We-RV is an RV repair shop in Pocomoke, Maryland, about half an hour from the Island. They also have a store in Chincoteague on Maddox Boulevard that carries parts and supplies. They'll send their service truck to your location 24/7. You'll find very good reviews from folks they helped.

- ✦ We-RV: 6631 Maddox Boulevard, Chincoteague VA 23336 (410) 251-0821, and 805 Ocean Highway, Pocomoke, MD 21851 (401) 957-1022 https://www.wervllc.com/ Email: wervllc@gmail.com

ISLAND VOICES

CHIEF R. K. FISHER AND CAPTAIN TYLER GREENLEY, TOWN OF CHINCOTEAGUE POLICE DEPARTMENT

Law enforcement isn't easy anywhere, but if that's your calling, Chincoteague might just be a good place to follow it. The town's original police station is a tiny structure next to the Island Theatre on Main Street built in 1942 and since converted to public restrooms. The department is quickly filling its modern headquarters in a more spacious location. I met Chief R. K. Fisher and Captain Tyler Greenley at the Oyster Festival, where they were in a positive frame of mind. "I'm not saying we have no crime," the Chief pointed out. "We have our share of incidents. But the Island is a very safe place." "We spend a lot of our time assisting visitors. We're able to do some positive things for the community, too," Captain Greenley told me. He listed a few: "The

Captain Tyler Greenley and Chief R. K. Fisher of the Chincoteague Police Department, at Oyster Festival 2021.

poker run. Little League. Flag football. We help at the Manna Café and deliver lunches to our seniors. We're able to assist the Fire Company. We like doing all of it."

"The Island has so much to offer," the Chief, a Chincoteague native, added. "I remember when every hotel from Dover, Delaware to the Chesapeake Bay bridge tunnel was full at Pony penning time. Now there are so many good places to stay right on the Island. We see a lot of people at the same time every year." He advises planning ahead for the beach. "That lot holds nearly 1,000 cars, but when it's full, people have to be turned away until space opens up. That happens often on the weekends. This year it happened for the first time on a weekday. We've seen a jump in traffic on Maddox Boulevard and backups leading into the refuge on Assateague, too. Remember, the launches of the bigger rockets at Wallops Island, such as the Antares, requires closing the beach for safety. It takes about two hours to get everyone off the beach."

Chief Fisher recommends an excursion to nearby Tangier Island if time permits. You'll have to go by boat. The ferry trip from Onancock (45 minutes from Chincoteague by car) takes about an hour. "It's a tiny place. People drive around in golf carts. Most everyone makes their living as a waterman. I like oysters OK, but I love crabs, and crabs are what they do best. Every Sunday, the women set up a huge family-style buffet in an outdoor pavilion. The price is low, and the food is outstanding." The Chief also appreciates the famous Tangier accent. "The speech of Tangier Islanders is like no one else's," he told me. "I could talk with them all day."

ISLAND VOICES

JACK TARR, FORMER MAYOR OF CHINCOTEAGUE

Jack Tarr, an electrical contractor and Chincoteague native, served as the town's Mayor for seventeen years. The license plate on his golf cart reads "FRMRMYR." He doesn't seem too unhappy about the "former" part. He had to stop and think for a bit when I asked him when his last term had ended. "Ours is the definition of grass-roots politics. It all starts at home," he pointed out. "I've seen my share of disputes. The old swing bridge came down, and the new one opened while I was Mayor. (It brings people into town by a different route.) People were split close to 50/50 on that and had strong

Jack Tarr, former Mayor of Chincoteague.

feelings about it. My advice to anyone in local government is to be honest. When you say you're going to do something, try to actually do it. When you sit down and talk to people about what you disagree on, it's often not as big a disagreement as you thought."

"It's tough to run a community that's so tourism-based," he added. "If you're stationary or stagnant, you're actually falling behind. You want to be growing. But growing pains are unavoidable. I try to think ahead ten years. That means you have to move forward with a plan." The desirability of the Island as a place to own a second home, or to retire, does create issues. "Many people downsize and move here from D.C. or other large places," Mayor Tarr noted. "It's safe. Taxes are low. And you're on "Island Time." But the cost of a home makes it difficult for young people starting out." Staffing local businesses has become a challenge recently. "We're busy five months of the year," the mayor noted. "Every vacation rental property is like a very small hotel, and that requires support services and people."

The Former Mayor is happy to see visitors enjoying the town and the Refuge. "We're the only beach on the East Coast with no development on it. Come visit. And come back."

We will.

ACKNOWLEDGMENTS

T O WRITE IS one thing; to be published is another. I'm grateful to Lawrence Knorr of Sunbury Press for his confidence in me, and his skill as an editor, since 2013. Crystal Devine created the thing of beauty you are holding (or viewing) from a simple document. Fen Alankus and Marianne Babcock were faithful guides. Thank you all. Many thanks to Darcy and Steve Cole of DSC Photography, who graciously permitted me to publish their glorious Island photos, the best possible way to bring the text to vivid life. My daughter Andrea devoted herself to capturing the portraits of the Island Voices 'Teaguers, full of truth about the people themselves. She shared in the journey of the creation of the Guide, as did her sister and brothers, and my wonderful wife. I could not love you more.

I'm grateful to the good people of Chincoteague who have welcomed and hosted our family for many years. There's no one quite like you. You're very good at what you do. Special thanks to those who took the time to tell me their stories, speaking from their hearts so others could see the Islands through their eyes. Thank you, Jonathan and Jane Richstein of Sundial Books, Chincoteague, for your warm hospitality for many seasons, and for advising me on the Guide as only the best sort of independent bookstore owners could do. I'm very grateful to Erick Sahler and Jim Duffy for reading the book before publication and offering such kind reviews, and to Nancy and John Cline for reading it aloud as it was being written, and offering such encouraging words. Thank you, Stephanie Skiro, for your unique vision.

God bless us, every one.

David Parmelee
February, 2022

ABOUT THE AUTHOR

DAVID PARMELEE is also the author of *The Sea Is a Thief* (Sunbury Press, 2013), a historical novel set on the Island of Chincoteague during the War between the States, and two chapter books for kids, *Miss Feesenschneezen Is Ill* (Sunbury Press, 2017) and *Miss Feesenschneezen is Fit* (Sunbury Press, 2020), based on little notes and cartoons he used to put in his 4th-grade daughter's lunchbox to make her laugh. Both are illustrated by Maria DeCerce. David is an actor, director, and playwright. His one-act plays *TOAST!*, *The Comment Section*, *Stan & Stella*, *Three Romances about Macbeth*, and *A Masked Ball (with Emotional Distancing)* have been produced by community theatres in Northeastern Pennsylvania. David and his wife Toni Jo Parmelee, D.O., are the parents of four children, each an incredible blessing, and have a marvelous granddaughter who figures quite prominently in *The Traveler's Guide*. David wishes for your time on Chincoteague and Assateague to be as joyful as his.

Made in the USA
Las Vegas, NV
31 January 2023

66588135R00095